The Scholars Mentor's Guide to Global Success

for International Research Students

Dr Agnieszka Piotrowska

The Scholars Mentor's Guide to Global Success for International Research Students

Copyright © *Agnieszka Piotrowska*, 2025
All Rights Reserved

The author, Agnieszka Piotrowska, asserts their moral and legal rights as the sole creator and copyright holder of this work. No part of this publication may be copied, reproduced, stored, or transmitted in any form or by any means—electronic, mechanical, photocopying, recording, or otherwise—without the explicit written permission of the author, except in cases of fair use for review, scholarly commentary, or citation with proper attribution.

All rights, including but not limited to reproduction, adaptation, translation, and public distribution, are strictly reserved. Unauthorised use or reproduction of this material is a violation of copyright law and will be subject to legal enforcement.

Contents

Preface 8

Chapter 1 10

Embracing the Journey 10

Chapter 2 42

Understanding the International Scholar Experience 42

Chapter 3 68

LEARN: Exploration of the Various Ways to Define and Understand Success 68

Chapter 4 101

LEARN MORE: Academic Success Strategies – feeling discouraged? 101

Chapter 5 118

LEARN AGAIN: Strategies for International Research Students to Cope with Depression, Homesickness, and Low Mood 118

Chapter 6 184

INSPIRE AND BE INSPIRED: How to move from 'the survive' to 'the thrive' mode 184

Chapter 7 197

ORGANISE; Developing a Growth Mindset 197

Chapter 8 208

ORGANISE MORE: Networking and Collaboration 208

Chapter 9 217

NAVIGATING THROUGH SURRENDER: Radical Gratitude: growth through challenging times 217

Chapter 10 232
NAVIGATE YOUR NEXT STEPS: Looking Ahead ... 232
Appendix 244
Additional Exercises: 244
REFERENCES 246

Acknowledgements

Every meaningful project is held up by more than one set of hands. It's nurtured, challenged, and inspired by the presence of others—those rare people who give generously of their time, insight, and heart. This book, like The Scholars' Mentor initiative itself, is no exception.

I want to express my deepest gratitude to the Advisory Board of The Scholars' Mentor, a group of extraordinary individuals who are not only distinguished colleagues but also dear friends. Each of them brings a wealth of experience, compassion, and vision to this work—and each one has helped shape the journey in ways seen and unseen.

In alphabetical order:
- Dr Jane Carr
- Dr Stewart Cornes
- Dr Charmaine Dambuza Kundai
- Dr Pete Dean
- Dr Babar Dogar Hussain
- Professor Tamara Dragadze, DPhil (Oxon)
- Professor Diana Jeater
- Professor Phillip Powell, PhD
- Helen Reade
- Dr Priyanka Singh

To this wonderfully diverse and generous circle, thank you. Your wisdom, care, and encouragement have enriched both this book and my broader mission to support international scholars around the world.

Preface

This book is based on my experience as a student, a PhD supervisor and as a life coach supporting doctoral students, globally, formally and informally, in English-speaking countries, mostly in the UK but also in the US.

The statistics regarding PhD completions in the UK and US say that 50% of those who start drop out. But even this frightening statistic is confusing and does not give you a full picture, which is more terrifying. When you first enroll in a PhD program, you're typically registered as an MPhil or MRes student, and about half of all candidates withdraw before passing their institution's required milestones. When I finished my PhD at Birkbeck, University of London, in 2012, there was only one threshold called 'an upgrade.' To complicate the completion figures, universities require students to clear two preliminary milestones before they can even be formally registered as PhD candidates. That means the real statistic for those who get the PhD but never finish it is a lot worse. In fact, around 75% of all those who start never finish. The volume aims to disrupt these statistics and offer you a better chance to succeed, using techniques outside the usual academic guidelines.

I will explore the background to some of the situations the international researchers find themselves in but I will also suggest mindfulness, growth and other holistic solutions to help you through your academic and life journeys. It is my aspiration that through working with this book, you, the Esteemed International Student, will not only finish your studies successfully and get the job of your dreams but also find your life purpose and the foundations for your lasting legacy.

Chapter 1

Embracing the Journey

Welcome, Gentle Reader, to a journey of transformation and triumph. This book is for you—the international research student or academic professional who has bravely crossed oceans in pursuit of knowledge and growth. It is a self-help holistic volume rooted in my own academic journey and that of my successful doctoral students and mentees. The book aspires to be more than that: drawing from a multi-psychological and intellectual background, including psychoanalysis, positive psychology, Lacanian psychoanalytically based psychotherapy and holistic life-coaching with elements of meditation, I present a way through the murky and often unspoken path, through the maze of the academic frustrations and deep lows which can affect anybody's mental health. My aspiration is that through reading this book, you will be able to step into your Light and emerge empowered and positive.

The LION™ Methodology and the process you will go through

The LION methodology and the process are simple but not easy, meaning you will still need to make an effort to understand the academic process, embrace some of the information and then take steps to remain positive and with high energy always on your side. I call this methodology a LION methodology, and it is created from the first letters of this simple philosophy below. The methodology is thus the following and can be divided into four stages:

1. LEARN. Learn and understand some of the academic knowledge pertaining to the educational situation you find yourself in. The facts and the context are not pleasant but are essential to know; for example, almost 70% of international students feel lonely, the same percentage drop out, the cultural landscape is different to what you are used to, people do not care as much as you thought they might. No need to be depressed, though: just know that this is what the context is in order to arm yourself and be prepared. There is nothing worse than imagining a land of milk and honey only to discover something completely different. Learn also about who you are, what your values are, and

what your true desires and then set your intention calmly and resolutely. Learn to get rid of your limiting beliefs and embrace new rules and new ways of being in the world.

2. **INSPIRE** – aim to inspire others and as well as be inspired. The global phenomenon coach Tony Robbins also advises us to 'give more than you expect to receive.' Understand some of the research on motivation and the description of culture and how one can deal with it. This will be supported by my sharing my personal experience of the academic journey both as a student and as a very experienced supervisor. Be INSPIRED too – nothing improves anybody's mood better than the knowledge that there are people who have been on this journey, succeeded and found their voice.

3. **ORGANISE** – during the Mindvalley training, which I completed in February 2025, there is a module called 'organise your mind,' meaning being aware of your thoughts and feelings in order to gain mastery over the way you see your life and, therefore, your general mood and ability to take action. Take some time to get to organise your mind and, of course, your surroundings.

Armed with that knowledge, gain awareness and follow self-care steps and meditation. This book will give you some tools to do this.

4. NAVIGATE, NEGOTIATE AND TAKE NEXT STEPS – Work towards your life purpose through different tools offered in this book, such as gratitude, including radical gratitude, empathy and curiousness and gaining more awareness – what is it you want to do in life and why? What are your core values? What are your fears, and how can you overcome them? How do you want to contribute to the world to make it a better place?

Through that approach, I believe that you will *manifest* your desired outcomes that will lead you to your life purpose–the degree, a good job, a good relationship – through the setting of clear intention and visualising the outcome, not just through some abstract mantras or boards but through taking clear steps to help you achieve your long-term goals.

Every chapter has plenty of exercises which you are encouraged to engage with. It is crucial to believe that the right path is there for you and that you will achieve your goals.

PERSONAL REFLECTION

Our past and our histories will, in some way, influence the way we think.

When I was a PhD student, I wished I had been offered this kind of support, but it was nowhere to be found. I subsequently provided versions of it to my own doctoral students, and here we are. The work on the book has also inspired my initiative, The Scholars' Mentor, and you are most welcome to visit the website and come to us for more support at www.scholarsmentor.com.

I have to add a disclaimer; clearly your progress and strength will develop better if you are working with a trusted coach. However, you can do a lot of work yourself and the work is mainly on developing your awareness and powerful presence in the world. The exercises included in the book are aimed to help you develop these techniques.

This is also a book which I have been asked to write by my own former PhD students, those who proudly present themselves as my mentees, but also a relatively large number of informal mentees from different disciplines who have asked for help and support over the years. The way this work has been conceived is to both offer an overview of the challenges and to give some tools and exercises for growth – these might be helpful for many people but an international researcher might find them particularly helpful.

The volume is not meant to be an academic treatise and so I have purposefully avoided complex references. However, I do want to begin by referencing a vital study which deals with the sense of loneliness experienced by international students. The study carried out by researchers and research students accessed a large sample of interviewees. It was carried out with the help of the BBC in the UK. Even though it mentions the qualitative methodology, its large sample gives it the weight of a quantitative as well.

The title of the article is: *The experience of loneliness among international students participating in the BBC Loneliness Experiment: Thematic analysis of qualitative survey data.*

The authors: Kangning Zheng, Sonia Johnson, Ruby Jarvis, et al.

First publication: The findings were first published in the journal *Current Research in Behavioral Sciences*, 2023

This study examines the experiences of loneliness among international students using data from the 2018 BBC Loneliness Experiment. It provides a qualitative analysis of *521* international students' responses, highlighting the multifaceted nature of loneliness.

1. **Themes Identified:**
   - **Negative Psychological and Social Aspects:** Emotional distress and challenges in social integration.
   - **Distressing Experience of Being Alone:** Feelings of disconnection, introspection, and geographical separation from family and friends.
   - **Disrupted Connections:** Difficulty forming meaningful relationships due to cultural and communication barriers.
   - **Entrapment:** A sense of helplessness and being trapped in loneliness.
   - **Stigma:** Shame and fear of judgment for experiencing loneliness.
   - **Positive Aspects:** A minority highlighted benefits like self-reflection and personal growth during isolation.

2. **Impacts of Loneliness:**

o   Loneliness significantly affects emotional health, well-being, and social functioning, limiting the benefits of overseas education for students.

o   Whilst some of these themes might be to be expected, the overall picture that it presents is disturbing. Clearly, one does expect more of the institutions hosting the students, and they do offer some services such as counselling for the international students, but there is a stigma attached to using these still. I will return to the need of using these services, though later in this volume.

Interestingly, the article does focus on policy recommendations (such as promoting social integration through culturally inclusive teaching methods and support systems, enhancing mental health services targeted at international students and so on). However, it does not suggest other tools, such as coaching and also self-help instruments, which might offer some help to the international student community, and those I feel are as important.

I hesitated whether it was a good idea to begin with such a depressive research paper. Yet, it is important to ascertain that the need for multiple support for international students is real and many strategies need to be deployed to create lasting help. Before I say anything else to you, the international researcher in a host country, do choose your doctoral supervisors very carefully and check how many 'completions' they have had (meaning how many doctoral students they have chaperoned through to the successful viva). This is a key piece of your decision-making as academics can be brilliant at their discipline but very poor at taking care of their supervisees. Yes, a life coach can help – but I personally have done too many 'hidden 'supervisions' – meaning really supervising somebody and not just looking at their well-being and resolve – that I know how hard it is if people who are leading you frankly do not know how to supervise anybody without thwarting their individuality or cannot engage with the emotional needs of their students. Often, it is simply due to the ever-increasing workloads and schedules that academics have. An expectation that on top of their teaching, research and administration, they also somehow have to become life coaches is simply unrealistic.

Meanwhile, you, the international student suffers. You come from vibrant cultures and carry within you the dreams of not just personal success but the aspiration to bridge worlds through understanding and communication. I am a great believer in education as a bridge and a pathway out of various cultural limitations and traditions, which, however amazing, can also hold us back. Some of these legacies are important to recognise and respect, but at times, we need to simply put them aside in order to succeed.

I (Dr Agnieszka Piotrowska) with a graduating student originally from Saudi Arabia

It is worth bearing in mind that doing a PhD in a foreign country is in itself an astonishing success. Dear Reader, if you are indeed such a student, be proud of your achievement already. And yet, we know the path is strewn with challenges—language barriers that silence your voice, cultural nuances that elude your grasp, and the weight of expectations that sometimes feel too heavy to bear. This book can be your compass, giving you the knowledge of the actual landscape, it offers some ideas as to how to guide you through these trials towards a horizon of success. It is designed as a source of knowledge and a journey of transformation, where your academic aspirations and personal growth converge.

I am your guide, a bridge-builder between worlds, having traversed the realms of award-winning filmmaking and the rigours of academia. My mission is to illuminate the path for international students and researchers, helping them to not only survive but thrive in their scholarly pursuits. Of course, my hope is that any student or researcher might find this volume of help.

With a track record of unwavering support for my cohorts and a near 100% PhD completion rate among my doctoral students, I bring a unique perspective that transcends traditional academic support. Together, we will unlock the potential within, fostering resilience. The book stems from my own experience as a PhD student, too, and I will share it with you henceforth.

My own PhD experience

My experience of doing a PhD quickly and efficiently in 3 years flat was, in the end, an extraordinarily rewarding one, but not without moments of real doubt and despair. I passed my viva with no corrections and was awarded a college distinction at the University of London in 2012, entered an academic career and became a full professor 8 years later. I have now stepped down from a full-time academic career as some of the ideas I have about PhD supervision are not aligned with the ethos of formal higher education. However, I am still formally supervising PhD students in the United Kingdom and also internationally.

It is important to say that I entered my doctoral journey as a mature student with plenty of successes behind me in my professional life, as an award-winning documentary filmmaker, specialising in making film portraits about people who perhaps were strange and extraordinary in some ways but who, under the surface were pretty much just like you and me.

I am mentioning this because my training in telling stories through film, but also theatre, and creative writing has empowered me to encourage some students and some coaching clients to re-write their narratives optimistically and positively, in other words, to find stories of triumph in ordinary situations in order to propel them forward.

Why I did the PhD in the middle of a super successful creative television career, including many award-winning documentaries and international awards and nominations, for example, an International EMMY, is perhaps a story for another day. Still, perhaps it is important to say that my whole family history did influence my decision to do a PhD – and I am sure it has also influenced yours. I will tell you about my personal history and my mother further in this chapter.

The direct decision for me to do the PhD was to do with my feelings that I was deeply uncomfortable about some mechanisms I observed on my journey as a documentary filmmaker: that is that people often opened up to be in my films because of a sense of a bond that was created between us during the process of the film production but with the intention being not to make their lives better necessarily but to create a spectacle that audiences would enjoy. It is because of that sense of unease that I studied for a Post-Graduate Diploma in Applied Psychology, which was illumination, and then decided to embark upon my transdisciplinary PhD, which combined psychology and film studies.

The title of my transdisciplinary project was *Psychoanalysis and Ethics in Documentary Film* –and it has, in due course, become a monograph now in its second edition (2014, 2023), published with one of the best academic publishers, Routledge. When I did a doctorate in early 2009, I wrote a basic PhD proposal, sent it out to several institutions in London and got accepted to all of them with some scholarship offers, too. I chose Birkbeck, University of London, because I wanted to work with two-particular world-leading scholars and psychotherapists. I was excited beyond description.

However, literally six weeks in, despite my maturity, life experience, successes and a plethora of friends ready to support me, I was ready to give up. An auxiliary (and inexperienced) person on the supervisory team made me feel discouraged, hopeless and depressed. I felt that the doctorate was a mountain I would not be able to climb. I marched to the office of the Director of the Graduate School, the wonderful Professor Lynne Segal, in floods of tears and told her I would leave the programme as I was made feel inadequate. Lynne felt it was such a bizarre turn of events as she thought I was very talented and came across as confident and knowledgeable. However, she could not really offer any strategies except for me to ask for the auxiliary supervisor to be removed asap. Even that encounter, of course, for anybody less confident, would have been a real challenge. Higher Education is deeply hierarchical, and nobody challenges or changes supervisors easily. I did, but it certainly was not easy or comfortable.

Looking back, I really do think I was close to abandoning the journey a few times that first year. There were a number of things in my toolbox I could use, not least the knowledge of psychology, but that was not the only thing. The strategies which I am aiming to share in this book and to replicate in my digital mentoring and coaching programmes too come in many guises. First, I did turn to personal psychoanalytically based psychotherapy. I was very lucky that I had the resources and the knowledge to ask for help outside the formal university system. I believe that it was important that it was not a part of the university in any way. I did not want any stigma of people thinking I was weak or, worse, somehow mentally unstable. Yes, the stigma of mental health was still there, and I believe this is still the case even today despite great progress being made. Also, because of the nature of my PhD, embarking on expensive psychoanalytically based psychotherapy and psychoanalytical training was easy to justify: I was not asking for help– I was simply embarking on a research journey to support my doctorate through additional psychotherapy and psychotherapeutic training. Second, I had an incredibly supportive circle of family and friends and a good peer group at the College. Still, I absolutely believe today that a real-life coaching experience would have been invaluable for me and indeed for you, too, going forward. I did not, at that point, do any visualising or manifesting exercises consciously. I did not know how to manifest, and my spiritual life, which was always there, was muddled. But I do remember sitting on the bench outside Birkbeck, my college, right in the middle of London, and imagining that I was grounded in the earth, with the roots coming from my body deep into the earth and with the light coming inside me and getting rid of all the despair and negativity. This is, of course, basic grounding and meditation, and I did it unconsciously. Some of the techniques I have learnt since I am sharing in this book in the shape of simple exercises at the end of each chapter.

Last, and that was important to me, my late father had passed away not long before that, and one of his last wishes was for me to do a PhD as he was an intellectual and an academic. 'You have such a good brain,' he used to say.

Do something with it which is more than telling tales about bizarre people.' There is also a whole story of my mother, who was a brilliant undergraduate student but whose ambitions for further study were never realised, for a variety of reasons, of which later. Some of the sections of this book deal with your desire as a doctoral student to embark on this journey. It often is not a straightforward situation and it is often that we have embraced our family's desire.

Childhood, Lost Opportunities, and the Power of Mentorship

Our childhood shapes us in profound ways, sometimes in ways we only fully grasp later in life. My mother's story has always lingered in my mind—not just as a reflection of her life but as a lesson in what support, or the lack of it, can mean for an individual's future. My own childhood took place in communist Poland, and its awfulness is something hard to describe and hard to convey – some films do indeed try to describe the horror of feeling you could not trust anybody ever.

This is my mother, Zofia, and me

Soon there will be only a small number of people who are currently young enough to remember all this without getting in despair, as it was pretty awful. At times, when I get back to Poland and meet some of my friends or colleagues who remember those moments first-hand, we do feel like dinosaurs of the historical times, which are gone, thank goodness, and seem so unreal and surreal. It almost makes us smile when people complain about the fake news, and 'the fake news' was the order of the day even as late as the 80s, even after the Solidarity movement, even during and post the Martial Law of 1983 when everybody should have known better but the media still carried on with the lies simply saying the economic and political situation was marvellous when there was only vinegar and cans of peas in shops. I guess the optimistic part of it is that the totalitarian regime did crumble. I guess we must take hope from these historical lessons. Things did change even when, at times, they seemed impossibly frozen and doomed to continue for millennia. I left early Poland – and how is really a different and pretty dramatic story left for another time – but I knew even then, as I do know today, that for me, given my family circumstances, to leave this was the only way to have a different life. Had I stayed, I would have been a pretty and possibly educated housewife and mother, at best, I fear. Maybe it is but a morbid fantasy, and in truth, one never knows what would have happened. But I do know what happened to my mother.

My mother was quite a brilliant woman in many ways. She was also rebellious and difficult – or so they said. She was the first woman in the family to get to the university, and her future was very bright. The story is long and complicated, but in essence, she got pregnant whilst still very much a student, did not finish her Masters, never mind any post-graduate qualifications, and somehow all her life tried to come to terms with the loss of her career opportunities, and maybe simply opportunities for her own development. How I know this story is not great, as parents should not tell their children that the pregnancy was unexpected and somewhat disturbing, and it disrupted the perfect flow of life. For the longest time, I was very angry about this, angry that I knew and angry that somehow, I felt I was blamed for my mother's decisions. In time, I have become grateful that she made a choice to keep the pregnancy, and me.

For years, I carried anger about this—anger that she shared her regrets with me, anger that I somehow felt responsible for her lost opportunities. Yet, in time, my perspective shifted. I came to recognise that her struggles were not merely personal; they were systemic. Women, especially in certain societies and time periods, were expected to choose between motherhood and professional aspirations. What if she had received proper guidance? What if someone had told her that it was possible to pursue both?

Years later, she returned to university and obtained her degree. But it was too late for it to make a real difference in her career. I often think about how different things might have been had she had a mentor who believed in her potential and helped her navigate the challenges of balancing personal and professional life.

As I reflect on my own journey, I recognise that mentorship is a powerful tool. Many international students, particularly those coming from backgrounds where opportunities are limited, face similar struggles. The fear of making the wrong choice, of not living up to familial expectations, of sacrificing one path for another—it can be overwhelming. This is where mentorship steps in. A good mentor does not merely offer advice; they offer belief and the conviction that one's dreams are valid and possible.

This is why *The Scholars' Mentor* exists. It is not just about academic success—it is about empowering individuals to navigate their paths without feeling forced to abandon parts of themselves. It is about making sure that no one has to look back with regret, feeling that their potential was lost to societal expectations or a lack of support.

My mother did not have that kind of support. But I hope that by sharing her story, I can be part of a movement that ensures others do. Childhood and upbringing shape us—but they do not have to define our limits. With the right guidance, we can break through the barriers that once seemed insurmountable, forging new paths toward fulfilment and success.

Why are you doing your PhD?

Do you know? Usually, people have a sense of a vague unease at the outset: they do not know. This realisation might make you feel uncomfortable, but one of the solutions I suggest is that you could think through your research topic at the beginning of your journey so that it aligns more with your own passions. This might seem a radical suggestion – and I will discuss it later- but it is better to change your path rather than abandon it.

With hindsight, despite being very settled in the United Kingdom and having been British for a long time by the time I started this doctoral programme, some of my difficulties at the start were exacerbated by the fact that, culturally, I was different from my British peer group and my British supervisors. Even my excellent Director of Studies made me feel at times that I was – well, unusual, to put it mildly, and at times straightforwardly weird.

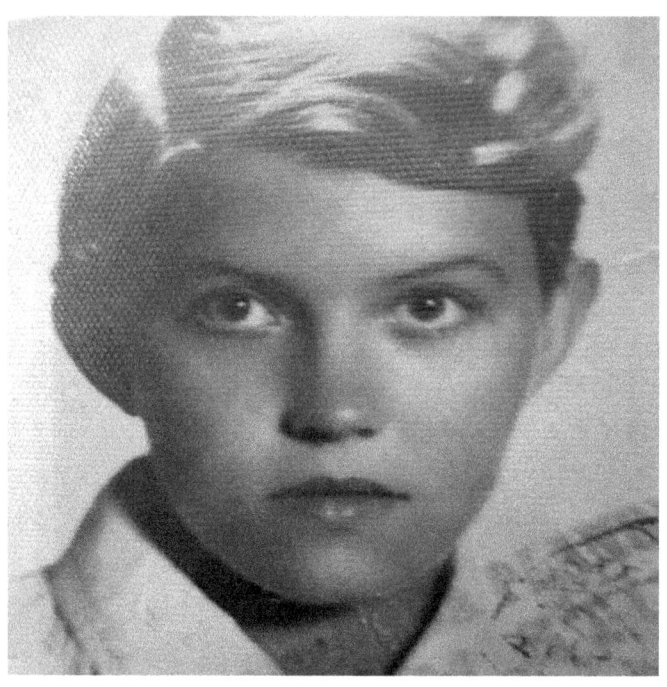

My mother, Zofia Lazarowicz, as a schoolgirl in Poland in the late 50s

He did not quite understand why some things mattered to me so much and why I would feel upset at times. I am writing this as a person who had lived up the road from the University, had a loving family locally, many London friends and peers, and generally should have simply enjoyed the journey without the pain. But the pain was there throughout. Everybody who has gone through the PhD – whether they are an international student or a domestic one will know that pain and the moments of darkness, but those whose origins stem from a different part of the world will feel the pain more acutely. Of this, there is no doubt.

This book aims to alleviate some of these moments and to suggest strategies for travel in ways which are joyous, productive, and ethical. How do you get the important qualification without giving up too much of who you are? How do we stand in our own truth without being made to feel somehow stupid and inadequate? Throughout this book, I share my experiences, interspersed with some academic research. But also, as mentioned, the volume has some basic holistic exercises, including simple meditations, which I invite you to engage with. I have found that the process of meditation will calm your mind and offer you clarity. Of course, I have never used it when I supervise my formal PhD students, but I have used it a lot in my life coaching practice, and the results are always outstanding. It is easier when somebody guides you, but you can learn to do it alone.

My own experience of supervising international students in the UK was pivotal in creating this book and the mentoring programmes. Armed with my own experience, my training in psychoanalytically based psychotherapy and my training as an educator and life coach, I decided all these years ago to be a different kind of supervisor to my PhD students, and I have always offered them support which extended beyond the scholarly research. This book simply builds on the strategies which they have found helpful. What was very clear is that students from different parts of various graduate schools working towards different goals in other disciplines (like math or economics) would reach out to the time to get emotional support and some strategies to deal with the sense at times of being so alone, isolated and just abandoned by various systems)

The book of course, might be of interest to anybody at all who is going through a PhD journey – not just international students.

The students are typically full of dreams and aspirations, but often, their host country can appear hostile. They can feel isolated and unsupported. They often feel under pressure to perform as their families may have sponsored their educational adventures. At times might struggle.

My own experience was hard, but not very hard compared to so many other people I knew. In my own PhD cohort (when I was a student myself), 50% indeed did drop out, and actually, they were, in fact, all British students.

Those coming from different parts of the world exclusively to study in a different land and often in English, which is not their first language, could find the journey unbearably hard. Language barriers impact communication and integration.

It is hard to say 'I am struggling' not only because of the academic pressures. There can be expectations from family and foreign institutions or even authorities who perhaps sponsored the academic journey. Whilst this volume is mostly aimed at PhD students, any international students might find it of interest for these reasons. I once had a female MA student from Saudi Arabia on a full scholarship from her host country, doing media studies and really struggling on every level. She was married, and her husband was studying too, but it was she who had to deal with the cultural expectations of looking after him, including cooking meals as well as doing her academic work. We tried to get her to write her dissertations precisely about cultural differences, including her choice to wear a veil at all times. She was a very successful MA graduate in the end, although she felt that the family pressures were too much for her to carry on – but of course, many women do. For this particular person, the MA was a great achievement, and I am very proud of her, too.

This experience has made me question many things, and I list below some of them:

-As an international student, how do you go through cultural adjustment and challenges without giving up completely the sense of who you are?

-How do you make the most of opportunities which present themselves in your host country and university without spending all your time seeking support from those from your own country?

-How do you deal with unexpected emotional challenges, feeling lonely and misunderstood?

-The research part and the discipline necessary to achieve your goal are but one thing. There are also the various thresholds looming ahead: the viva and then finding a job.

I will be offering strategies coming from my background:

- Recognising the unique challenges: Addressing language barriers, cultural adjustment, academic pressures, and emotional challenges.

- Thinking through and identifying your aspirations: Outlining the desire for academic success, personal growth, and effective integration into new cultural environments.

In the quiet corners of bustling university libraries and the silent pauses of online classrooms, I've witnessed the unspoken challenges you face. You, the international student, have crossed oceans and time zones in pursuit of knowledge, only to grapple with the unexpected emotional toll of cultural dissonance and academic pressure. This book is born out of a deep empathy for your journey and a recognition of the urgent need to address the challenges that, if left unchecked, can lead to a spiral of self-doubt and isolation, hindering the bright future you are working so. There are exercises at the end of each chapter which will help you with the following:

- Gain a profound sense of self-awareness and authenticity in your academic and professional journey.
- Develop resilience and effective strategies to navigate cultural and academic challenges.
- Learn to maintain motivation and enthusiasm, transforming stress into a catalyst for growth.
- Acquire enhanced communication skills for a successful cross-cultural engagement.
- Build a strong foundation for future career opportunities and personal development.

My aim is to help you discover the keys to not just surviving but thriving in the complex tapestry of international academia. This book is your compass to chart a course through the stormy seas of cultural adjustment and academic pressures, guiding you to a place where your voice is not just heard but resonates with confidence. Together, we will turn the challenges into stepping stones for a fulfilling and transformative journey.

In this book, I will also present some stories from my own experience as an educator and just a person. I will also present findings and academic research ideas regarding international research students. In the exercise sections, I will invite you to embark on a transformative journey together. It begins with a thorough assessment, where I'll help you uncover the layers of your unique academic and cultural challenges. I have listened to your stories – or people going through a similar journey- ensuring that your experiences are the foundation upon which we build your path to success. As we move forward, you'll find inspiration in creative solutions that reignite your passion and guide you through the intricacies of your journey. Finally, we'll nurture your growth, aligning your academic achievements with the aspirations that resonate with If you choose to work with me through my coaching platform, we can deepen the process, but you can do a lot of this work on your own or with a trusted friend.

-the difference between your desire and your intention. Does it matter? How does it matter? What can you do to align the 'desire' and the 'intention'?

We begin by exploring deep into the reasons why you have embarked on the PhD journey at all. What was your desire? Where did it come from? Is it truly your desire or that of your family? In other words, why are you doing it at all? In my own case, and I believe in the cases of many other PhD candidates, it was a combination of things: I was very curious to think through the mechanism of the process which was taking place between a filmmaker and the subject of her film, that is the person that she is making the film about and I truly wanted to take time to explore psychoanalytical always of thinking about the process, which in due course led me to 'transference' a powerful unconscious mechanism that takes place often in any asymmetrical power relationship where one person is in some position of power and authority.

My PhD was about 'transference' out of the clinic and how it can be used unethically in documentary filmmaking but also in other spheres of life including indeed education. 'Transference' is simply a deep attachment you feel for your doctor and psychotherapist, but also anybody in a position of power and authority, including your educator and your supervisor. This, therefore, can be used for the good. But it can also have very negative consequences when you, as a student begin to feel inferior to your supervisors and almost anybody else. It's important to grab these emotions before they become a real obstacle.

Your supervisors and peers are not superhuman but, at times might appear so. A powerful example of 'transference' which can have catastrophic consequences is what's known as the Stockholm Syndrome, where those who are kidnapped or held hostage develop positive feelings akin to love towards their captors. Nobody is saying that this can happen in a university environment. However, there are still confused and complex circumstances, particularly when you are not surrounded by your support network, your friends and family.

We will examine the challenges of cultural differences. To what extent do they matter? (They do). How do we manage not to feel depressed when our academic supervisors make us feel disrespected? Perhaps they are just trying to help – or perhaps they, too, are scared and exhausted.

We will look at strategies that will lift your low mood and even depression, and learn how to analyse our own emotions and feelings and why journalling might be a helpful tool. And what about empathy? How could we deploy it to forgive some harshness and get more disciplined?

Finding joy and peace, which can make us more effective in our academic work and in life, can be achieved by all the above but also by quiet meditation.

We will consider the power of spiritual tools and coaching, which will include believing in a higher purpose and doing your research for the highest good of all.

All these ideas and others will be presented in the ensuing chapters. The overriding aim of the work is to motivate you to reflect on what it is that you want to do in life, why, and how you can make the world a better place. Researchers are uniquely positioned to influence their students as well as the academic and other communities. I hope when you find what I call 'life purpose,' you will find happiness, success and a way to make a positive contribution to this troubled world we live in.

I wish you all the very best in your academic work, in your research, your career and also in your life.

May the Light be with you.

Agnieszka Piotrowska, PhD
Founder, The Scholars Mentor
www.scholarsmentor.com

Chapter 2

Understanding the International Scholar Experience

A few years ago, I had an Egyptian colleague at a university I worked at. She was extremely accomplished both as a scholar and a teacher. But because of her cultural background, she was perhaps louder than a British counterpart would be. Also, in particular, she used to wave her hands around a lot. A complaint was lodged against her for being too aggressive. She was a senior professor, so the entire story eventually blew over, but her difficulties resulted in her moving to a university in the Middle East. Another research student (whom I only coached post his failed viva) had similar challenges and ended up having to resubmit his thesis for reasons to do with his cultural presentation rather than his knowledge or the value of the work he produced. This felt so unjust and unfair. It was all fine in the end after I supported him, but he should never have been made to feel this way. I will go through some fundamental challenges here before exploring this situation and possible remedies further.

Let me then set the stage for our further discussions and exercises.

The international scholar experience is a unique journey filled with opportunities, challenges, and profound personal growth. As you navigate through this path, it's essential to embrace the transformative nature of your time abroad. This journey not only enriches your academic pursuits but also builds resilience, adaptability, and a deeper understanding of diverse cultures. By acknowledging the complexity of your experience, you can pave the way for a fulfilling and successful academic career while forging meaningful connections that span the globe. It is a wonderful experience to step into one's light and one's authenticity, so it is doubly important that this does not end.

Cultural adjustment plays a pivotal role in the international scholar experience. Moving to a new country often involves navigating unfamiliar customs, languages, and social norms. This transition can be daunting, but it is also an opportunity to expand your worldview and enrich your personal identity. Embracing the local culture, participating in community events, and seeking out support networks are integral to easing this adjustment. By cultivating an open mindset, you not only enhance your academic journey but also foster a sense of belonging that can significantly impact your overall well-being.

Stress management is another critical aspect of the international scholar experience. The pressures of rigorous academic demands, combined with the challenges of adapting to a new environment, can lead to overwhelming stress. It's essential to develop effective coping strategies that promote mental well-being. Techniques such as mindfulness, regular physical activity, and establishing a balanced routine can help mitigate stress. Additionally, seeking resources available on campus, such as counselling services or workshops, can provide valuable support, allowing you to thrive both academically and personally. However, these resources will never be enough if your mindset is not set to be positive and growing which is your own responsibility and your own project which this volume is assisting you with.

Work-life balance is often a delicate dance for anybody and for international research students. It can be a particular challenge. The pursuit of academic excellence can easily consume your time and energy, leaving little room for personal interests and social interactions. However, achieving a harmonious balance is crucial for long-term success and satisfaction. Setting clear boundaries, Prioritising self-care, and scheduling time for leisure activities can rejuvenate your spirit and enhance your productivity. Remember, a fulfilled scholar is one who nurtures both their academic ambitions and their personal passions, creating a holistic approach to life and learning.

Ultimately, understanding the international scholar experience is about embracing the journey with all its complexities and triumphs. Each challenge faced and each connection made contributes to your growth as a scholar and as an individual. By cultivating resilience, seeking support, and maintaining a focus on your mental well-being, you can navigate this experience with confidence and clarity. Your journey is not just a means to an end; it is a rich tapestry of experiences that will shape your future and inspire those around you. Embrace every moment, for they are the building blocks of your success. Remember to put aside time daily to visualise your success and feel happy and confident about it, even in moments of crisis.

The Role of a Life Coach within the Academic Environment

Nobody talks about a life coach as a tool to support your doctoral journey – and yet this might be a crucial part of your development as a researcher, as a scholar and as a person. I would argue any excellent supervisor has to be a bit of a life coach and a counsellor. In this day and age, when higher education institutions struggle under economic and time pressures such an ambition is not something most institutions can deliver. There are, of course many questions here and the financial one as well: can a research student afford a life coach? Currently, the universities in the UK, US and Australia at least do offer some kind of counselling service but not at all a life coaching one. The difference between the therapist and a counsellor is huge (although there are some similarities as both practices must, of course, be client-centred). Many therapists and counsellors still shun powerful questions and even hesitate to set up future goals, not to mention the additional alternative strategies such as grounding and meditation. And believing in stepping into the Light. And yet I believe these are important in anybody's wellbeing.

The journey of an international research scholar is often filled with unique challenges and opportunities that can shape their academic and personal lives. In this intricate landscape, a conversation with a life coach can serve as a guiding beacon, illuminating the path toward success. By providing tailored support and strategies, life coaches can empower students to navigate the complexities of academia while fostering resilience and adaptability. This transformative relationship enables scholars to embrace their potential fully, cultivating a mindset focused on growth and achievement.

Let me be very clear here – I do believe that you can empower yourself with the help of your friends and family, perhaps the university counselling services and indeed with the help of this book, for example, and other resources. However, it will be harder, and if your supervisor does not see themselves as a 'life coach' of sorts or is too busy, for example, you might start feeling abandoned and rejected. It is in these situations that a life coach can play a pivotal role in helping international students develop effective academic success strategies. Through personalised sessions, coaches can assist scholars in setting clear, achievable goals that align with their research aspirations. It is both the encouragement to create concrete steps and routines but also offers holistic support, including meditations and spiritual support – if you have the right coach. By fostering accountability and providing constructive feedback, life coaches help students stay motivated and on track, transforming overwhelming tasks into manageable milestones that boost confidence and competence.

Setting Intentions for Success

Setting an 'intention' for success is a powerful first step for anybody. For international research scholars embarking on their academic journeys, it is a crucial step. 'Intention' serves as guiding principles that clarify your goals and aspirations, providing a roadmap that leads you toward success. By setting clear and purposeful intentions, you harness your energy and focus on what truly matters, allowing you to navigate the challenges of academia with confidence and resilience. As you immerse yourself in new cultures and environments, having a defined sense of purpose will not only enhance your productivity but also enrich your personal growth. Again, the idea of setting an intention comes from the New Age ideas of energy healing. Still, whether you are a fan of thinking about existence in terms of energy flows or not, it is clear that to get anywhere, you must know where you are going and why.

To effectively set intentions, begin by reflecting on your core values and what success means to you. This self-exploration is essential as it helps you align your intentions with your personal and academic goals. Consider the specific outcomes you hope to achieve during your research journey. Do you aim to publish your findings in reputable journals, develop meaningful collaborations, or contribute to the academic community in a unique way? By articulating these aspirations, you create a vision that inspires and motivates you, transforming abstract goals into tangible intentions that can guide your daily actions.

All the above sounds important and, of course, right, but there is one core question which you need to ask yourself first: why are you even doing this PhD at all? Why have you arrived in this foreign country and a foreign city? There is not great need to feel embarrassed and anxious is this was perhaps not exactly your desire but that of your family! Your desire cannot be discovered yet, and it needs to be discovered if you are going to succeed in this journey.

Look at the topic carefully again and ask yourself whether you might actually be interested in something somewhat different. If this sounds like an unusual idea let me tell you that all my 10 PhD students who have completed their doctoral studies changed the title of their research in the first year – sometimes quite dramatically, other time times perhaps substantially. The exercise of sitting quietly at the very beginning of the journey and asking what it is that you really want to do might save you and your supervisors a lot of heartache not to say suffering in due course. I had one student who embarked on a thesis looking at the importance of technology in developing narratives in his home country (Pakistan). He ended up with a beautiful and important thesis on the issue of masculinities in Pakistani cinema. These topics, whilst connected, are, in fact, completely different, but the student who is now a fully-fledged academic with some publications to his name took time to really try and discover what his true desire might be. You will never complete anything well – and perhaps you might not complete it at all – if your heart is not in the project. It is here, too, that a life coach might be able to help establish your true potential interests and passion – and that passion cannot be a desire to get an academic job – it has to be more than this. It has to be an ignited dream which you will carry in your soul through many a dark night.

As you define your intentions, it's crucial to frame them positively and in the present tense. Instead of saying, "I want to complete my thesis," rephrase it as "I am successfully completing my thesis and gaining valuable insights to do good in the world, as well as to improve my life and that of my family." "I am working towards getting a successful academic job." This shift in language reinforces a mindset of success and empowers you to take ownership of your journey. Visualise your intentions regularly, incorporating practices such as meditation or journaling to strengthen your commitment. By consistently reminding yourself of your intentions, you cultivate a positive mental environment that fosters resilience and determination, essential traits for overcoming the hurdles of academic life.

A collage of myself with my research students, some of whom now serve on The Scholars' Mentor Advisory Board (Dr Priyanka Singh and Dr Babar Hussain)

In addition to individual intentions, consider how your goals can harmonise with those of your peers and the broader academic community. Collaboration is a cornerstone of research, and aligning your intentions with those of your colleagues can lead to collective success. Engage in open discussions about your aspirations, and be receptive to the visions of others. This collaborative spirit not only enriches your own experience but also fosters a supportive network that can help you navigate cultural adjustments and the complexities of academic life. Together, you can create an environment that celebrates shared achievements and mutual growth.

Finally, as you progress on your research journey, regularly revisit and reassess your intentions. The academic landscape is dynamic, and your goals may evolve as you gain new insights and experiences. Embrace this fluidity and be willing to adapt your intentions to reflect your current circumstances and aspirations. This adaptability is a crucial skill for international scholars, enabling them to balance the demands of research, cultural integration, and personal well-being. By staying attuned to your intentions and nurturing them throughout your academic journey, you position yourself not only for success but for a fulfilling and transformative experience that extends far beyond the classroom.

Understanding the Significance of One's Personal Desires

Knowing and understanding our personal desires is really important. In the context of a PhD as well, it is essential to find your own motivation in terms of why it is important for you to engage in research. Whether your reason is a romantic one or is supported by self-determined and rational choices, it does not matter. It is only this feeling that is able to sustain you while engaged in research, where institutional choices dominate quantities of work and shape content.

Separating superficial motivations from real feelings underneath is fundamental. This is not the 'me first' of the ego but an attempt to understand the principle of behaviour. The main research aim is to have a ring of truth when feelings come through, resonate, and provide a greater perspective. One has to reflect on one's own feelings. At the end of the first solo meeting I had with one young colleague, he was left puzzled and expected a reaction and a justification for the choice he made. It is not for me to offer a solution.

Clarifying and Dissecting True Motivations

This perspective suggests that clarity about one's personal motivation for starting a PhD project matters.

Hence, I think it is worthwhile to clarify these motivations and critically reflect upon them. From my experiences, I have learned that many PhD researchers struggle with the expectations they put on themselves and the goals and visions they actually have. Very often, questions like 'Who do I want to be?', 'What does success mean to me?' or 'What are my core values?' are not explored in the academic world at all. Moreover, I think that these questions can potentially guide my research and ensure that it is in line with my aspirations. I might lack critical thinking due to my inexperience in the field of business administration, but I am certain that one's attitude and motivation have a significant effect on the decisions people make and on their will to achieve goals.

Dissecting motivations for a journey of this nature is important, and asking some basic questions might help: Why did I apply for a PhD study? Without overthinking, the initial answer can give us a first idea of our primary motivations. Personally, I like to gather various perspectives in order to identify a certain phenomenon's complexity. I think that this strategy helps me deal with risks. By thoroughly reflecting on our answers to the question mentioned above, we can grasp whether we are driven by intrinsic or extrinsic motivation. It is vital to reflect critically upon our mentors' advice and to question whether we are more inclined to pursue a PhD study because of external pressures or due to our own attitudes and visions. Suppose our decision to undertake a PhD stems from ourselves. In that case, we have a better chance of withstanding potential difficulties and staying true to our academic as well as personal aspirations.

And let's be clear here – any desire is a combination of a variety of things. It is possible to develop and genuine passion, even if it is a combination of family aspirations, talents, opportunities and so on. The important thing is to recognise these calmly and develop the intention to carry on well and purposefully in small but resolute steps, moving forward towards your goal – possibly with the help of a coach. The alternative is a feeling of being unmotivated and even being dishonest somehow. Unless this is honestly resolved, a situation can lead to mental health issues.

Assessing Personal Feelings and Emotions

As emotions are unconscious components of our thinking, a resource for motivation, cognitive function, and decision-making, personal feelings need to be not only recognised but also assessed, especially when it comes to motivation and overall well-being. A plethora of complex and nuanced feelings that are consequently related characterise life as a PhD student including both bad and good days, general well-being, and different levels of work productivity. Therefore, engaging in regular self-assessment of these feelings can significantly enhance finding information, identifying underlying issues, and finding effective solutions in order to overcome low productivity, disorientation, and stress in study and research. Embracing this self-assessment practice and exercises is a powerful tool. Please consult the exercises at the end of this chapter, but in essence, find time to sit quietly and ask yourself what you want and why.

Visualise your success, bearing in mind that your own vision of success might be different from that of your parents or wider family. Close your eyes and sit still, listening to your breathing and ask yourself simply: 'What is my vision of success?' It is also helpful to have small tasks and big tasks and goals listed in your own mind. What does 'abundance' (that fashionable word) mean for you? Is it just the financial benefits or perhaps a success in your personal life, with a loving family and friends?

An essential question to answer is how to effectively assess these feelings. A first, but nonetheless essential, way of doing this is through maintaining a journal and engaging in reflective practice. By consistently writing down feelings and experiences, PhD students not only become more critical towards their own emotional state but also develop a knack for critical analysis and synthesis. Consequently, this heightened sense of self-awareness enables them to resist being easily discouraged and proactively seek appropriate support and guidance.

Emotions are linked to thoughts, which are obviously linked to motivation. Thus, positive feelings can put your mind in a more productive state and enable you to be highly motivated. At the same time, negative feelings have the power to reduce one's capability. For this reason, I would suggest that emotional intelligence can be as important as traditional intelligence in predicting a person's success and happiness. Emotional intelligence is something you can learn and develop through becoming aware of how you feel and what you can do to change these feelings. Emotional intelligence, in this sense, will allow you to know your feelings and have the strength to work through them in order to approach life in a calm, strong, empathic, and polite manner. Psychologists have tried to understand the role of emotions in the regulation of our moods, how they may be regulated, and what kind of consequences emerge. Therefore, to put it most simply, you need to understand your emotions and gain control over your moods to develop resilience and overcome challenges. Emotional intelligence modulates emotions, regulating different feelings, their motivational significance, and the cognitive processes related to their organisation and meaning structure.

Navigating Challenges and Overcoming Obstacles

A research journey is filled with both highs and lows as you navigate towards key milestones. During these times, your personal motivations will be challenged, and it may feel as though your drive is being tested. There will be moments when your progress feels like it has stalled, and your sense of hope may fade. But it's in these moments that the strategies you develop to cope with obstacles will prove crucial. Staying committed to your research, your intention, and your desire and reaffirming your goals will keep you moving forward. The strength of your motivation is what will allow you to reconnect with your purpose and continue the work. Your emotions play a significant role in shaping your motivation. When you understand this, you can also identify areas where you might need support. Confusion may leave you feeling lost, while a crisis could make you want to point fingers. Recognising these emotional responses will help you find clarity and keep moving forward.

There will be times when your ambitions feel so large that it seems like obstacles are constantly in your path. It can be hard to assess or make sense of the situation when you're in the midst of an intense struggle. Nothing seems to be going according to plan, and it can feel as though everything is working against you. But this isn't necessarily a setback—it's actually an essential part of the process. These moments, when everything feels difficult, help shape your resilience and test whether your ambitions are truly worth pursuing. While it may seem discouraging at times, remember that ambition is about more than just achieving a goal—it's about testing, learning, and reaffirming your path as you move forward. These struggles are part of what will make your success even more meaningful.

Dealing with Confusion and Overwhelm

If your intention is set clearly and resolutely (for the highest good of all), and you remember to ground yourself regularly, hopefully, the feelings of confusion and overwhelm will become less frequent. However, your journey naturally involves dangerous stretches. You may not yet have all the answers, and how you approach your work will depend on so many personal factors. Your personality, your strengths and weaknesses, your preferences for specific research methods, and even your state of mind all influence the way you navigate your research. In addition, factors like the research tradition you are a part of, your career goals, your ethical beliefs, and countless other personal elements play a role in shaping your approach.

It is essential to accept that this is part of the process. The ups and downs, the frustration, and the emotional rollercoaster are all part of the journey. You might feel frustrated at times—and that's okay. Can you make space for that frustration and allow yourself to acknowledge the emotions behind it? Embrace where you are, knowing it's all part of the growth and learning process.

Here are some practical things you can do:

- Divide big objectives/tasks into smaller ones according to a feasible order of doing them; ---confront uncertainty: plan and program the work to be done and the time to accomplish it; -ask your friends, colleagues, thesis supervisors, and co-supervisors for help, reason, or a friendly chat;

- Sometimes, push yourself against discipline until the chaos inside you becomes familiar (at least less chaotic) and, in some cases of PhD research, turns into order and your scientific mission.

The Role of Intrinsic Motivation in Sustaining Doctoral Research

'Intrinsic motivation' to achieve is the cornerstone of embarking on a PhD. Those who are intrinsically motivated to research are more successful. What is this 'intrinsic motivation'? A deep, abiding interest in the subject matter predisposes an individual to a willingness to expend what is termed "deep attention" in terms of thorough and profound engagement with the material. If you are lucky enough to really do your research and your studies out of a deep commitment to your study area and not for some other external reasons 9 family ambitions, society's expectations, etc.), then it is so much easier to carry on with the journey. Given that the completion of this thesis is but one aspect of achieving the long-term goals associated with undertaking a doctoral program, things that can make it also deeply and abidingly satisfying are intrinsically rather than extrinsically based. That is, external motivators such as money, security, accolades, and enjoyment are all based on others affirming one's work, all changeable external conditions. Satisfaction in the present rather than prospective future conditions is believed to create personal success and wealth and is particularly valuable in arts management. People are attracted to the field because they love the subject matter.

The extrinsically motivated student creates for themselves exactly the conditions necessary to reinstate in their lives what has really struck them as being missing by going through the experiences of attaining each and every highly qualifying research accolade. To truly love the process leads to successfully and sustainably having the outcome, if it is meant to be, in a resilient manner. Resiliency and determination, some of the valuable aspects of high motivation, are necessary character traits for any doctoral student because of the significant personal, emotional, cognitive, and practical pressures placed upon candidates.

Identifying and Cultivating Intrinsic Motivations

Supporting research claims that the onset of a PhD is the most challenging period for many research students. Why is this? It is argued that many students begin their doctoral study driven by *extrinsic* motivations rather than identifying and being clear about what really motivates them intrinsically to conduct PhD research. Thus, it is suggested that research students should start their doctoral journey by identifying, developing, and nurturing their intrinsic motivations in doing research. Subsequently, these inherent motivators can be used later on to keep the personal motivation of doctoral students high throughout the entire PhD research period and beyond.

How do we know what our intrinsic motivators are? If this sounds repetitive, then please forgive me, but there is no shortcut here: you can only gain self-knowledge through deep introspection. By undergoing a process of self-reflection, you can explore the following: 1. Interests/Passions – students should identify what really interests them and what they are passionate about in their research area. It is argued that our enthusiasm is where our passions and interests are. Staying enthusiastic can be a result of sticking with our passions. In this vein, the staying power of enduring the journey is where our pursuits align with what one is passionate about.

In other words, we are looking for 'joy' in your journey. And looking for 'joy' in the journey is almost synonymous with looking for, and finding the most valuable thing of all – our life purpose. What makes you truly happy? When have you felt you have really fulfilled your ambitions but also positively contributed to the world?

It is, of course, easier said than done perhaps, but a series of well-designed practices such as meditation, journalling, and visualising exercises, as well as being with people who make you happy rather than somehow confused or depressed will, in the long term, result in your being able to find joy in your heart and then in your soul. Some people find their life purpose early on in their life journey and they are the lucky ones. This achievement – finding your life purpose – is what you really want to see in your research journey, and it is that achievement, rather than any degree, that will matter most to you.

Concluding reflections

Establishing the intention and the personal motivation for pursuing a PhD is indeed an urgent matter for any doctoral student. These are the steps to finding your absolute joy and your real purpose in life.

Through a lifelong journey of exploration, I have found that any PhD demands not just intellect but also spirit. Just as wisdom marries state-of-the-art knowledge, a successful doctoral journey is made of both intellect and the identification of personal desire. One could say that any success at all involves the 'desire' and the ' intention' working side by side. Knowing what it means to combine the two in order to feel genuinely excited and enthusiastic about the journey is a sign of maturity and the closeness of being able to arrive at the knowledge of what your purpose in life might be,

Meditative and Visualisation Exercises

Grounding with Inner Light

Sit comfortably in a quiet space. Close your eyes and take three deep breaths, inhaling deeply through your nose and exhaling slowly through your mouth.

Visualise roots growing from your feet into the earth, anchoring you firmly to the ground. Feel the support and stability of the earth beneath you.

Imagine a warm, golden light entering through the top of your head, filling your body with a sense of calm and energy. Let the light expand, surrounding you like a protective shield.

As you bask in this light, visualise your goals clearly. This is what setting an intention is. You want to achieve much – not for yourself only but also for the world. See yourself achieving these goals step by step. Hold onto the feelings of pride and joy this brings. Stay in this space for a few minutes before opening your eyes.

The Mountain Visualisation

Sit upright and close your eyes. Imagine you are a tall, strong mountain. Feel the unshakable stability and strength in your body as the base of the mountain.

Visualise the challenges in your life as passing clouds. Watch them drift by without attaching to them. Know that as a mountain, you remain grounded and resilient, no matter the weather.

Bring your goals into focus. Imagine them as the peak of your mountain. Reflect on the path you are taking to reach them and how your strength and stability will guide you.

Light Path Meditation for Goal Setting

Find a comfortable seat and close your eyes. Breathe deeply, letting your body relax with each breath.

Visualise a path of light stretching out before you. This is your journey toward achieving your goals.

Step onto the path in your mind's eye. Notice the details: What does it feel like to walk toward your dreams? What obstacles do you see, and how do you overcome them?

At the end of the path, see yourself achieving your goal. Imagine the details of this success—what it looks, sounds, and feels like. Let yourself experience the joy and pride fully.

Heart-Centered Meditation for Empathy

Sit quietly and close your eyes. Place your hands over your heart and take slow, deep breaths.

Imagine a soft, green light radiating from your heart. As you breathe, let the light grow, filling your body and surrounding you with warmth and compassion.

Bring to mind someone difficult in your life. Imagine them surrounded by this green light of empathy and understanding. Reflect on what challenges they might be facing and how you can approach them with kindness.

Hold this visualisation for a few minutes, then release it with gratitude for the insight it provided.

Chapter 3

LEARN: Exploration of the Various Ways to Define and Understand Success

Personal vs. Academic Success

Personal success and academic success, while often intertwined in any walk of life, are linked to each other. But, clearly, you can be happy and live in a tent on a beach somewhere with no academic degrees. One could say that personal success encompasses the holistic growth of an individual, including emotional intelligence, resilience, and interpersonal relationships – but even that might simply be trying to find categories where there are none.

You could say that personal success has to be about finding your voice, understanding who you are beyond your scholarly pursuits, and cultivating a life that aligns with your values and passions. It is about finding your life purpose. Whether you are an academic student or a personal who has lived on the same street all their lives. You must learn what are your actual values. There are many techniques to do this – one of them would be writing down a list of 15 qualities you admire: courage, discipline, boldness, intelligence, creativity, and enthusiasm, but there could be others like obedience, modesty, diligence and so on. Then reduce these to 10 =, then to 5 and 3, and see what you get: mine are love, creativity and courage. Therefore, when things come my way that really grind against these, I will be unhappy. My life purpose is indeed to bring these qualities to the lives of my students, my clients and my mentees.

On the other hand, academic success is often measured by tangible outcomes such as grades, publications, getting through milestones and the completion of research projects. It requires strategic planning, time management, and a commitment to continuous learning. By setting clear goals and actively seeking mentorship and resources, these scholars can position themselves for success in their academic pursuits. However, it is crucial to recognise that academic achievements should not come at the expense of personal well-being.

The intersection of personal and academic success is, therefore, a complex matter, and it has to link back to your intentions, desires and life purpose. If your life purpose is catching fish for people to eat, then perhaps doing a PhD is not necessary. So – does doing this PhD make you truly happy? Do you know why you are doing it? These questions have to be asked over and over again.

Generally, it is true to say that when international research scholars prioritise their mental well-being and cultivate meaningful relationships, they create a supportive environment that enhances their academic performance. However, the question still remains if this will make them happy.

Stress management techniques, such as mindfulness and physical activity, can significantly improve focus and productivity. Generally, whilst a small amount of stress is simply an element of life, it is also possible to be overstressed and burnt out.

Please remember that your mental health is just as important as your academic achievements. By addressing stress and maintaining a balanced approach, you can navigate the rigours of their academic journey more effectively.

As already suggested, cultural adjustment plays a vital role in the success of international scholars. Adapting to a new environment can be both exhilarating and overwhelming, leading to feelings of isolation or anxiety. Scholars need to engage with their communities, seek out cultural experiences, and connect with fellow students. Building a network of support not only fosters a sense of belonging but also nurtures personal growth. As scholars share their experiences and learn from one another, they enrich their academic journeys and contribute to a more vibrant scholarly community.

Understanding Cultural Differences

Cultural differences can vary widely from one part of the world to another. This can and does matter in university settings. Students come to universities from diverse locations and cultures. They must learn to respect and work effectively with people of different worldviews. This begins with recognising the wide variety of cultural differences in the world. Some areas of possible cultural differences in educational settings include general philosophies of management, pedagogical theories, and behavioural expectations of professional educators.

My former PhD students, now members of the Advisory Board dog the Scholars' Mentor: Dr Priyanka Singh, Dr Babar Hussain, Dr Charmaine Dambuza, and myself, having a moment of relaxation and joy

Cultural Dimensions Theory

Dutch researcher Geert Hofstede developed this theory in 1980 after surveying over 100,000 IBM employees from 50 countries. The theory identifies several dimensions that help explain how different societies prioritise and navigate social behaviours. In his study, the 'culture' is understood in a broad sense – not just geographically or ethnically defined, but rather 'culture' across society's classes and different lines too, such as a sense of belonging to customs and habits, religions and ethnic groups.

Cultural Dimensions Theory is a general framework which is frequently cited in the context of the internationalisation of higher education. Central to this theory is the development of six dimensions, each representing an underlying characteristic of societal culture and its influence on individual behaviour, values, and communication preferences. The dimensions include the following:

- Power Distance (PD) measures how inequalities in power and authority between people are perceived and accepted by members of society.

- Individualism (IDV) versus collectivism (COLL), reflecting the tendency of individuals to either look after themselves and their immediate family members only or to belong to wider social groups—tribes, organisations, communities, or nations—and act in favour of those groups' interests even when personal interests may run counter to this.

- Masculinity (MA) versus femininity (FEM), which reflects the relative importance of work and the role of money that society attributes to both males and females.

- Uncertainty Avoidance (UA), which reflects the extent to which people feel threatened by or feel the need to control uncertainty and ambiguity. Such a need is motivated by perceived threats or the stress of the unknown.

- Long-term Orientation (LTO) versus short-term normative orientation (STNO). In spite of the controversy in the academic community over the validity of the differences in the fifth dimension, LTO tends to reflect values focused on future rewards, such as saving, hard work, and perseverance.

Hofstede's Cultural Dimensions

Power Distance Index (PDI)

| High: Acceptance of a hierarchical order in which everybody has a place and which needs no further justification. | Low: People strive to equalize the distribution of power and demand justification for inequalities of power. | |

Individualism versus Collectivism (IDV)

| Individualism: As a preference for a loosely-knit social framework | Collectivism: Tightly-knit framework in society. | |

Masculinity versus Femininity (MAS)

| Masculinity: Preference in society for achievement, heroism, assertiveness and material rewards for success. | Femininity: Stands for a preference for cooperation, modesty, caring for the weak and quality of life. | |

Uncertainty Avoidance Index (UAI)

| High: Maintains rigid codes of belief and behavior and are intolerant of unorthodox behavior and ideas. | Low: Societies maintain a more relaxed attitude in which practice counts more than principles. | |

Long Term Orientation versus Short Term Normative Orientation (LTO)

| High: Pragmatic approach, they encourage thrift and efforts in modern education as a way to prepare for the future. | Low: Societies prefer to maintain time-honored traditions and norms while viewing societal change with suspicion. | |

Indulgence versus Restraint (IND)

| Indulgence: Societies that allow relatively free gratification of basic and natural human drives related to enjoying life and having fun. | Restraint: Societies that suppress gratification of needs and regulates it by means of strict social norms. | |

74

Understanding these societal dimensions and their interaction can provide faculty and students insight into their own value systems, as well as those of others. When misunderstandings or conflicts do arise, consideration for such differences in perception can reduce tensions and open up routes to greater understanding among students. Institutions can work to use these five dimensions of cultural differences to help develop positive cross-cultural relationships and increase the potential to resolve conflicts that arise as a function of misunderstanding cultural differences. Research has shown that cultural dimensions can influence academic behaviours among students, such as academic motivation, preferred learning style, academic knowledge, attitudes toward talking and writing, and tolerance of ambiguity. As learning in teams and groups becomes enshrined in higher education, understanding the implications of such terms on academic collaboration becomes increasingly important, enhancing the capacity of educators and students to achieve the intended benefits of cross-cultural and intercultural arrangements in educational practices.

Cultural Differences: Navigating and Thriving in University Settings

Be proud of your heritage! But do understand that at the same time, international students and domestic students from international families and communities can experience cultural differences within the university setting, which can feel unexpectedly alienating. These differences lie in three areas: communication style, attitudes towards authority, and approaches to learning. In countries where education is viewed as a collectivist endeavour, such as many Asian countries, students in the classroom frequently engage in group study and group exams. In countries like Canada, the US, and the UK, individual effort is recognised and even awarded; group work is often seen as an end rather than an end in itself. This can lead to friction in project groups.

Learning about differences can be rewarding and inspiring. As an educator in higher education in the United Kingdom and internationally, I have always insisted that students and researchers from different countries work together. My doctoral students, whilst doing their own projects, attended seminars in which their different approaches to life were shared, as well as their research projects. At Scholars' Mentor, we organise group containers which make people more confident and happier. I do remember well, though, running an undergraduate course at a UK University in which there was a massive misunderstanding among the Chinese students regarding what was expected and how they were meant to get from A to B.

In non-Western countries, students ensure they understand their course material by taking extensive, copious notes. They then study these notes to understand the content of a course. In Western countries, we generally rely more heavily on the spoken word and independent study. This can be a source of anxiety and misunderstanding. At a postgraduate level, students often take this to another extreme and become isolated in order not to appear 'needy.' Note-taking is not such a big part of the classroom dynamic. Whilst this, of course, is more relevant on an undergraduate level, it can also matter at the postgraduate and a research level. This can mean that Asian students mistakenly feel that the new learning environment gives them more free time and mistakenly believe that the workload is less; it is not. Many members of the South Asian community are accustomed to using non-verbal communication techniques to keep face, meaning that everything is okay when, in fact, it is not. Knowing this can help you avoid confusion and possible friction. The campus is a microcosm of the world. As with the larger society, beings from various corners of the globe—both culturally and literally. Knowledge and recognition of these differences will set the stage for respectful discourse and dialogue. This will lead to a better learning environment. Being proactive will increase one's confidence in resolving issues at the "front end" before they become problems. So:

- Be polite but bold at all times

- If you are not sure what is going on, do ask your tutor or your supervisor. Do not be shy, and do not assume

- Be open to different ways of seeing the world and smile at everybody! It works wonders

- Be prepared at whatever level that you will be expected to do a lot of work on your own

Stepping into a new identity – embrace it!!!

When you first step onto a new campus, far from home, the excitement and anticipation of starting your academic journey are often mixed with a sense of unease. For international students, the challenges go beyond just adjusting to a different university. You're not just facing the typical transition of being away from home for the first time—you're navigating a complex web of academic, social, and emotional hurdles.

Embarking on a research journey at a university abroad is like setting sail on a vast ocean, where the shores of your home culture and the new land of your host culture beckon. As a research student, you stand at the crossroads of these two worlds, each offering unique treasures and challenges. To truly thrive and succeed, it's essential to honour and integrate both. Your new identity is your past and your future, and it is necessary to create something new and be open to new possibilities.

Imagine you're a seasoned sailor accustomed to the familiar winds and currents of your homeland. The rhythms of your native culture have shaped your approach to learning, communication, and problem-solving. These ingrained habits and perspectives are your compass, guiding you through the academic seas. However, as you chart a course toward the host culture, new winds blow—different academic expectations, diverse social norms, and unfamiliar ways of thinking. At first, these may seem like turbulent waters, but they hold the promise of new horizons.

Not everybody will agree with this, but in my mind, the key to navigating this journey lies in embracing both cultures. I have seen over and over again students either trying to forget completely who they are or just being unable to move on from their traditions and then as a result of these strategies, failing. Neither of these strategies will work long-term. By acknowledging and valuing the strengths of your home culture, you bring a unique perspective to your research, enriching the academic community. Simultaneously, by immersing yourself in the host culture, you gain new tools and insights that enhance your scholarly endeavours. This dual embrace fosters a sense of belonging and identity that is both rooted and expansive.

Universities should play a pivotal role in this voyage. They are the sturdy vessels that can support you through the waves. Institutions that recognise and celebrate the diverse backgrounds of their students create an environment where all can flourish. This involves not only providing resources and support systems but also fostering a culture of inclusivity and mutual respect. When universities validate and appreciate the experiences of their students, they lay the foundation for a community where everyone can contribute and grow. However, more and more in the current neo-liberal climate, institutions may not feel that it is their job to create a supportive environment for their students, international ones and others. They still produce a chance to learn, and you, of course, must take that chance, but you may need to look for support and nourishment elsewhere.

As you embark on this academic adventure, remember that the journey is as significant as the destination. Embrace the winds of both your home and host cultures, and let them guide you toward success. I will repeat that being bold and tolerant at the same time can be tricky, but is the key to happiness and success.

Navigating Cultural Differences on the oceans of life!

As you navigate your journey as a research student, you're not just learning about your field of study—you're also stepping into two distinct cultural worlds. The first is the culture you bring with you, shaped by your home country, and the second is the new culture of your host university and the academic community you're joining. To truly thrive, you need to step into both these worlds, embracing your roots while also immersing yourself in your new environment.

It's a delicate balance, isn't it? On the one hand, you carry the rich tapestry of your cultural background with you—your values, your communication style, and the ways you approach problem-solving and learning. These elements of your "home culture" are powerful tools that have helped you navigate the world so far. But now, you find yourself in a new setting where expectations, social norms, and academic approaches might differ significantly.

At this moment, it's essential to embrace both cultures—not just one or the other. There is wisdom and strength in your home culture that can guide your academic journey, but there is also a wealth of knowledge, insight, and opportunity in the host culture of the university. If you only hold on to what you know, it can be like trying to steer a ship with just one oar—you're missing the full power of both perspectives.

Imagine you're navigating through uncharted waters. You're at a crossroads where your home culture and the host culture of the university converge. Think of the knowledge from both cultures as the wind that fills your sails, driving you forward. The home culture offers stability and familiarity, while the host culture presents new challenges and perspectives that help you grow. By embracing both, you will not only adapt to your academic surroundings but also enrich your own research, perspectives, and sense of identity.

For you as a student, this is an invitation to take part in that exchange. Be open to learning the new ways your host university operates, but also find ways to integrate your own unique experiences into the learning process. Participate in workshops, attend multicultural events, and connect with other students who are navigating the same journey. And remember, this is not just a one-way street. Your home culture can offer fresh insights that enrich the university's culture as well.

Your story—woven from both the past and the present—will be one of success, resilience, and an ever-

Accountability and Responsibility: The Heartbeat of Your Academic Journey

As you embark on the challenging yet transformative journey of research, accountability and responsibility are two of the most critical companions you'll have by your side. In academia, they are not just words but pillars that hold up the very structure of success. Responsibility, born from accountability, is a trait that can empower you to take control of your own learning, engage with your academic community, and ultimately chart your own path forward. It's the quiet force that drives you to show up—day in, day out—even when the waters get rough.

In academia, setting goals that are fuelled by your true desires is a powerful act. These intentions, driven not just by what you think you *should* do but by what you *want* to do and give to the world, offer you the courage to step into your fullest potential and find your life purpose. When you engage with your academic work this way, your motivations transform. They no longer feel like they are obligations or tasks to complete. Instead, they become an integral part of who you are, pushing you to break through barriers and rise to new heights.

It's here, within this realm of intentionality, that the student-mentor relationship finds its strength – inside the university or outside through an experience life coach like the ones provided by Scholars' Mentor. Mentors are not there to simply guide you through the academic maze—they are there to nurture your growth to help you understand that your success and failure are not just the result of chance but of the intentional actions you take. You are not just another student in a lecture hall; you are an active participant in your own learning. And it is through this participation, through taking responsibility for both your achievements and setbacks, that you will unlock the doors to your true potential.

Imagine yourself as a thriving and confident academic and, indeed, a human being who belongs effortlessly to whichever community you choose to be in. Visualise that picture in your mind through a series of meditations when you go for a walk or a run. Keep telling yourself, 'I am grateful for the opportunities I have been given and the achievements I have already accomplished.'

This is a journey that is deeply personal yet intrinsically connected to the academic community you are a part of. As you work towards your goals, you will find that the world around you begins to support you in unexpected ways. Whether it's through the resources available at your institution or the encouragement from your peers and professors, there is a network of support waiting for you to tap into. But here's the key—you must take the first step. You must show up, own your place in this journey, and make the most of the opportunities that present themselves.

But responsibility doesn't stop with your academic work alone. It extends into your personal growth, your emotional well-being, and the strategies you employ to stay grounded throughout this process. It's about learning how to manage the anxiety that inevitably comes with significant challenges. It's about finding peace amidst the chaos, whether through these practices - meditation, reflection, or through physical exercise or a collaboration with a life coach. The mindfulness practices — the meditations, walking and observing your thoughts, grounding in daily practice - are not mere luxuries—they are essential tools for sustaining your well-being and keeping you aligned with your goals. I return here yet again to a discussion of the desires and the intentions, from a different viewpoint, that is, from the perspective of responsibility and accountability. Once you have identified these, you need to own them and stand by them. Once you have done this lovingly and respectfully through your mindfulness practices, you will be well on a journey to finding your life purpose, which, in the end, is all we want and need.

Your motivation is as much about desire as it is about intention. Desire is the quiet voice that calls you forward, urging you to explore new territories, to stretch beyond what you thought was possible. And intention? Intention is the map that guides you along the way, ensuring that you stay on course even when the path becomes unclear. The beautiful balance between these two is what will carry you through the ups and downs of your research journey. When you are intentional about your desires and desires about your intentions, you have the recipe for success.

And remember, this journey is not linear. There will be moments of doubt, of missteps, and of re-evaluation. That's okay. It's all part of the process. The key is to stay engaged, stay curious, and never stop seeking the path that aligns with your deepest self. Suppose you can embrace both your desire to grow and the responsibility of shaping that growth. In that case, you'll find that your success as a researcher will not only be measured by the academic accolades you earn but also by the person you become in the process.

Implications for Practice

As you embark on your research journey, it's essential to recognise the profound interplay between desire and intention. These two forces are not merely abstract concepts; they are the very lifeblood of your academic and personal growth. Understanding and harmonising them can transform your experience, leading you to not only achieve success but thrive in ways you might not have imagined.

Desire: The Heart's Compass

We have already discussed 'intention' and 'desire' earlier in this volume. Clearly, without these you will have never left your bedroom and never embarked on this journey. Here, we look at the concepts of desire and intention from the point of view of a spiritual journey, which is part of your development, in my view.

Desire is the spark that ignites your passion. It's that inner yearning that propels you forward, urging you to delve deeper, to question, and to seek understanding. This isn't just about wanting to complete a thesis or earn a degree; it's about a profound longing to contribute to the world, to make a difference, and to find meaning in your work. This desire is deeply personal and often rooted in your unique experiences and background.

For international students, this desire is often intertwined with the aspiration to bridge cultures, bring diverse perspectives into the academic fold, and enrich the global community. It's about honouring your heritage while embracing new ideas and methodologies. This duality can be both challenging and enriching, as it requires you to navigate and integrate multiple cultural frameworks.

Intention: The Guiding Star

While desire fuels your passion, intention provides direction. It's the conscious decision to transform your desires into actionable steps. Intention is about setting clear, purposeful goals and committing to the path that leads you there. It's the roadmap that guides your journey, ensuring that your actions align with your deepest aspirations.

In the academic realm, intention manifests as the dedication to rigorous research, pursuing knowledge, and the commitment to scholarly excellence. It's about making deliberate choices that reflect your values and objectives. For international students, this might involve adapting to new academic standards, engaging with diverse methodologies, and contributing to a multicultural academic environment.

The Synergy of Desire and Intention

When desire and intention are in harmony, they create a powerful synergy that propels you toward success – in harmony and alignment with the Universe. It is my view that a belief that you are not alone, that there is a greater power, which is a power for the good. Even if you were to say you do not believe in God, you can imagine that the Universe wishes you well – and see the difference it will make to your life. Desire without intention can lead to aimless wandering, while intention without desire can cause a lack of motivation. Together, they form a dynamic duo that drives you to not only meet your goals but to exceed them.

This spiritual dimension and this synergy are particularly crucial for international students who are navigating the complexities of studying abroad. The challenges of adapting to a new educational system, understanding different cultural norms, and building a support network can be daunting. However, by aligning your desires with clear intentions, you can navigate these.

Your Journey Ahead

In conclusion, the interplay between desire and intention is the cornerstone of a fulfilling and successful academic journey. By understanding and aligning these forces, you empower yourself to navigate the complexities of research with purpose and passion. Remember, this journey is uniquely yours, and embracing both your desires and intentions will lead you to a place of profound personal and academic fulfilment.

Creating an Inspiring Vision Board to Guide You on Your Journey

My former PhD student, Dr Priyanka Singh, now at the University of Leeds, took my guidance and made up a cardboard credit card which said Dr Priyanka Savita 9. She was not married at the time. She said many times that looking at it made her determined and happy. Do that too.

When things seem difficult and discouraging, building a vision board is a transformative exercise that can significantly enhance your journey as an international research scholar, adding some light and hope as well as concrete action steps. It serves as a powerful visual representation of your goals, aspirations, and dreams. As you navigate the complexities of academic life, a vision board can help to crystallise your ambitions, providing a constant reminder of what you are working towards. This process not only engages your creativity but also allows you to focus your energy on the milestones that matter most to you, fostering a sense of purpose amidst the challenges of cultural adjustment and integration.

To begin creating your vision board, dedicate time to reflect on your personal and academic goals. Consider what success looks like for you in both your research and your life as a scholar. Write down your aspirations, whether they pertain to publishing your work, establishing meaningful connections within your academic community, or achieving a balanced lifestyle. As you articulate these goals, envision how they align with your broader life vision. This foundational step will guide you in selecting images, words, and symbols that resonate with your journey and inspire you to take action.

Once you have a clear understanding of your goals, gather materials that will bring your vision to life. You can use a traditional corkboard, a poster, or even a digital platform, depending on your preferences. Collect magazines, printouts, or personal photographs that embody your aspirations. Choose quotes that uplift and motivate you. As you arrange these elements on your board, allow your intuition to guide you. There is no right or wrong way to create a vision board; it should reflect your unique journey and the essence of who you are as an individual and a scholar.

Displaying your vision board in a space where you will see it daily is crucial for maintaining your motivation. This constant visual reminder will encourage you to stay focused on your goals, especially during times of stress and uncertainty. Each time you glance at it, take a moment to visualise yourself achieving those dreams. This practice of visualisation can enhance your mental well-being, helping you to combat feelings of isolation or overwhelm that often accompany the international academic experience. It can also serve as a conversation starter, allowing you to share your aspirations with peers and mentors, thereby fostering a supportive network.

Finally, remember that a vision board is not a static creation. As you evolve in your academic and personal life, so too should your vision board. Regularly revisit and update it to reflect new goals and aspirations that emerge from your experiences. This dynamic approach will keep you aligned with your journey, reminding you to celebrate your accomplishments while remaining open to new opportunities. Embracing this continual growth mindset will empower you to navigate the complexities of your research journey with resilience, clarity, and a renewed sense of purpose.

This is myself with my former PhD student Dr Charmaine Dambuza Kundai. We are now firm friends and collaborators.

Exercises leading to the Creating Vision Boards for Academic Success

Practical Steps to Align Desire and Intention

1. **Self-Reflection:** Take time to understand what you truly desire from your academic journey. Reflect on your passions, values, and long-term goals.

2. **Set Clear Intentions:** Once you've identified your desires, translate them into specific, measurable, and achievable goals. This will provide you with a clear direction and purpose.

3. **Seek Support:** Engage with mentors, advisors, and peers who can offer guidance and support. They can help you stay focused and provide valuable insights.

4. **Embrace Flexibility:** Be open to adjusting your intentions as you grow and learn. The academic journey is dynamic, and flexibility allows you to adapt to new opportunities and challenges.

5. **Cultivate Resilience:** Understand that setbacks are a natural part of the journey. Cultivate resilience by viewing challenges as opportunities for growth and learning.

Exercise 1: Visualising Your Doctoral Graduation and Beyond

Introduction:

Visualisation is a powerful tool for achieving your goals. This exercise will guide you through a meditation designed to help you imagine yourself at your doctoral graduation, confidently stepping into your future as an academic. You'll also visualise yourself working with students and publishing research. This process will help you create a vivid picture of success that can fuel your motivation and drive.

Meditation and Visualisation:

1. Find a quiet space where you won't be disturbed. Sit comfortably with your feet flat on the floor. Close your eyes and take three deep breaths, inhaling deeply through your nose and exhaling slowly through your mouth.

2. Begin by imagining yourself at your doctoral graduation. Picture the ceremony—the gown, the cap, and the feeling of accomplishment as you walk across the stage. See yourself receiving your degree and feeling immense pride in this milestone.

3. Now, visualise your future as an academic. Imagine yourself working with students—mentoring

them, guiding them through their research, and seeing them grow. Picture yourself teaching a class, presenting your ideas, and watching your students succeed.

4. Visualise yourself publishing your research. Imagine seeing your work in journals, being referenced by others, and knowing that you have made a lasting contribution to your field.

5. Spend 5-10 minutes in this visualisation, fully immersing yourself in the feelings of accomplishment and purpose.

6. After the visualisation, write your reflections:

o What emotions came up during this exercise?

o How did visualising your academic success help you feel more motivated?

o What specific steps can you take to make this vision a reality?

Reflection:
Reflect on the experience and write about any insights or emotions that surfaced. How does it feel to see yourself succeeding in your academic journey? How can you stay connected to this vision as you move forward?

Exercise 2: Creating a Physical Vision Board for Your Academic Journey

Introduction:

A vision board is a tangible representation of your goals and aspirations. By creating a vision board, you can bring your dreams into focus and provide yourself with a visual reminder of the academic success you are working towards. This exercise combines creativity with intention, helping you clarify and stay aligned with your goals.

Steps to Create Your Vision Board:

1. Gather materials: You'll need a poster board or large piece of paper, magazines or printed images, scissors, glue or tape, and markers or pens.

2. Reflect on your goals: Take a few moments to think about your vision of academic success—graduating, publishing, teaching, mentoring, etc. Write down keywords and phrases that represent your goals.

3. Begin cutting out images and words that resonate with your goals. Look for pictures of graduation, teaching, research, publishing, and any other photos that align with your vision of success.

4. Arrange the images and words on your board in a way that feels right to you. There's no right

or wrong way to do this—just let your creativity guide you.

5. Once you're happy with the layout, glue or tape the images onto the board.

6. Write any affirmations or goals that will keep you motivated. These can be succinct statements like "I am a published scholar" or "I mentor the next generation of researchers."

7. Keep your vision board somewhere visible, where you can see it daily. Let it serve as a reminder of the path you're on and the goals you're working towards.

Reflection:

After creating your vision board, take a moment to reflect:

- How does it feel to see your academic journey laid out visually?
- What emotions came up as you selected images and words for your board?
- How can you use this vision board to stay motivated and focused on your goals?

Exercise 3: Understanding and Embracing Cultural Approaches

Introduction:

As an international scholar, you will encounter a variety of cultural approaches to research, teaching, and academia. Understanding and embracing these cultural differences will not only enhance your experience but also empower you to work through challenges and build meaningful relationships with colleagues and students.

Steps to Understand and Accept Cultural Differences:

1. Reflect on the cultural background you come from. Write down three key aspects of your culture that influence your academic perspective or work. This could include communication styles, attitudes toward authority, or approaches to research.

2. Think about a time when you encountered a cultural difference in academia. How did you react? Write about this experience and how it made you feel.

3. Now, consider how you can approach cultural differences with greater empathy. What assumptions might you have made that could be reframed?

4. Write down one example of a cultural approach or practice from a different country or region that you admire or would like to understand more deeply.

5. Think about how you can incorporate this understanding into your own academic journey. Perhaps it's through a more open-minded approach to collaboration or a willingness to explore alternative research methodologies.

6. Practice patience and openness, knowing that embracing diversity in thought and practice will enrich your own academic and professional life.

Reflection:

Reflect on the cultural differences you've encountered in your academic journey. How have these experiences shaped your perspective? How can you continue to grow in your understanding and acceptance of these differences?

Chapter 4

LEARN MORE: Academic Success Strategies – feeling discouraged?

Mastering Time Management: A Pathway to Academic and Personal Success

As you journey through your academic life as an international research scholar, you quickly realise that time is one of your most precious resources. With a schedule filled to the brim—research projects, coursework, teaching duties, personal responsibilities, and the added complexity of cultural adjustment—finding balance can often feel like a monumental task. Yet, time management is not just about getting through each day; it is about crafting a space where you can thrive, both in your research and in your personal life.

The good news is there are techniques that can help you regain control over your time, reduce the stress that often comes with academic life, and create room for growth and well-being. By mastering these strategies, you set yourself up for success, not just academically but also emotionally and physically.

The Pomodoro Technique: A Strategy for Focus and Recharge

One of the most powerful time management tools you can incorporate into your routine is the Pomodoro Technique. This technique is deceptively simple yet remarkably effective. It encourages you to break your work into focused intervals, typically 25 minutes long, followed by a short 5-minute break. This process not only allows you to maintain high levels of concentration but also prevents burnout by giving your brain the rest it needs to perform at its best.

For you, as an international scholar juggling the demands of academic life, this method is particularly valuable. It's a way to structure your day into manageable chunks of work while also providing much-needed moments to recharge. These intervals not only enhance productivity but also make your academic journey feel less overwhelming, giving you the ability to focus on one task at a time, without feeling like you are constantly on the go.

Prioritising Tasks: The Eisenhower Matrix

Another indispensable technique is the Eisenhower Matrix, a method for prioritising tasks that will help you focus on what really matters. By categorising your tasks into four distinct quadrants—important, important but not urgent, urgent but not necessary, and neither urgent nor essential—you can easily determine where to invest your time and energy.

For international students like yourself, this is particularly helpful. The demands of academia, combined with the pressure of adjusting to a new culture, can often make everything feel urgent. But not all tasks require your immediate attention. The Eisenhower Matrix helps you take a step back, assess your priorities, and decide which tasks should be tackled first and which ones can be scheduled for later. This clarity is essential for achieving your academic goals without sacrificing your mental health and personal well-being.

Dr Charmaine Kundai's graduation celebration in 2022, which I attended as Guest of Honour.

Setting SMART Goals: Turning Ambitions into Action

Effective time management is also about setting clear, actionable goals. Using the SMART criteria—Specific, Measurable, Achievable, Relevant, and Time-bound—you can turn vague ambitions into concrete plans. As an international scholar, this means setting both academic and personal goals that are aligned with your values.

By making your goals clear and achievable, you can break down what may seem like an overwhelming journey into smaller, more manageable steps. Whether it's finishing a paper, mastering a new language skill, or simply finding time to connect with others from your home culture, these goals provide you with a sense of direction and purpose. They help guide your daily actions, ensuring that everything you do is in service of your broader vision of success.

The Power of Flexibility: Embracing the Unexpected

Finally, no matter how well you plan, life as an international research scholar is perhaps more unpredictable than you are used to. The challenges of living in a new country, coupled with the stresses of academic life, can sometimes throw you off course. This is where flexibility comes in. Being adaptable with your time management strategy allows you to pivot when things don't go according to plan.

Whether it's adjusting deadlines, changing study environments, or taking a break to recharge, flexibility ensures that you're not locked into a rigid system that causes more stress than it alleviates. By embracing this flexibility, you not only protect your well-being but also enhance your ability to respond to the dynamic nature of your life. This adaptability is key to maintaining balance and resilience throughout your academic journey.

Integrating Desire, Intention, and Time Management

In addition to setting intentions and identifying your desires, effective time management is an essential skill that will help you thrive in both your academic work and personal life. The Pomodoro Technique, Prioritisation strategies like the Eisenhower Matrix, SMART goals, and flexibility in your approach are all tools that will guide you through the complexities of being an international research scholar. By embracing these techniques, you create a well-rounded approach to time management that helps you not only excel in your studies but also cultivate personal growth and well-being.

Remember, time management isn't just about checking tasks off a list—it's about finding a balance that allows you to live and work with purpose, focus, and joy. When you align your desire, intention, and time management strategies, you set yourself up for a successful and fulfilling academic journey.

Whilst this volume focuses mostly on the mindset it is perhaps helpful to point out the necessary academic tools.

Finally, prioritise your mental well-being throughout this process. Writing can be a source of stress, particularly when faced with deadlines and the pressure to publish. Incorporate stress management techniques into your routine, such as mindfulness practices, regular exercise, and time for relaxation. A balanced approach will not only improve your writing quality but also contribute to your overall academic success. Remember, strong writing skills are not just about the words on the page; they are a reflection of your journey, resilience, and commitment to sharing your knowledge with the world. Embrace this journey with passion and perseverance, and you will undoubtedly succeed.

Embrace the Power of Awareness

The first step in navigating these differences is to cultivate awareness. Take the time to learn about the various cultures represented in your academic environment. This awareness is more than just recognising visible differences; it's about understanding the subtle factors that influence communication, work ethics, and social norms. Engage in open dialogues, attend cultural events, and immerse yourself in workshops that introduce you to new perspectives. By fostering a sense of curiosity and respect, you'll transform potential conflicts into opportunities for collaboration and personal growth. Each cultural encounter you experience enriches the academic community, making your journey more meaningful.

Building Relationships Across Cultures

Building strong relationships across cultural lines requires patience and intentional effort. Approach these interactions with an open mind and the willingness to adapt. Miscommunications may arise, and that's okay—these moments don't have to be setbacks. Instead, view them as valuable learning experiences that can strengthen your connections. Focus on effective communication: speak clearly, listen actively, and ask for clarification when needed. By doing this, you can bridge the gaps that cultural differences might create. Remember, trust and mutual respect are the foundations of fruitful relationships, and these relationships can lead to innovative ideas that enhance your research.

Achieving Work-Life Balance

Finally, work-life balance is a continuous process that benefits greatly from an understanding of cultural expectations and norms. Different cultures have varying perspectives on work, leisure, and family, and being mindful of these differences can help you better navigate your own responsibilities. Set clear boundaries, prioritise your tasks, and allow yourself time to relax and engage in social activities. As you integrate cultural insights into your daily routine, you'll find that they not only enhance your academic experience but also contribute to a richer, more fulfilling life.

Embrace the journey of navigating cultural differences, for it is a path that will lead to both personal growth and academic success.

Building a Support Network

Building a support network is an essential step for international research scholars to navigate the complexities of academic life in a foreign environment. I have already mentioned how, as an educator, supervisor and life coach, I often created these support containers with individuals from different cultures. The journey of pursuing advanced studies can often feel isolating, particularly in a new culture with distinct academic expectations. However, establishing a robust support network can not only ease the transitional challenges but also enhance your academic experience and personal well-being. This network can consist of peers, mentors, faculty members, and even local community organisations that share your interests and values.

Connecting with fellow students is one of the most effective ways to create a support network. Engaging with peers who understand the unique challenges of being an international research scholar fosters a sense of camaraderie and shared experience. Participate in study groups, join academic clubs, or take part in social events organised by your institution. These interactions can lead to lasting friendships and academic collaborations, providing both emotional support and practical assistance during your research journey.

In addition to academic connections, exploring local community organisations can provide an enriching layer to your support network. These organisations often offer resources and social gatherings that help you acclimate to your new environment. Engaging with local residents and fellow international scholars can broaden your cultural perspective and foster a sense of belonging. This connection to the community not only alleviates feelings of homesickness but also enhances your overall well-being, creating a more balanced life as you pursue your research goals.

Finally, remember that your support network is a two-way street. While you seek guidance and companionship, be open to offering your support to others as well. Be generous. Sharing your experiences and knowledge can foster deeper connections and create an atmosphere of mutual encouragement. By actively participating in your support network, you contribute to a thriving academic community that champions resilience, collaboration, and success. As you build these relationships, you will find that they not only serve your academic pursuits but also enrich your personal journey, empowering you to navigate the challenges and triumphs of being an international research scholar.

Celebrating Diversity in Academia

Celebrating diversity in academia is not just an ideal; it is a powerful reality that enriches the educational landscape. For international research scholars, the myriad perspectives and backgrounds represented among peers serve as a catalyst for innovation and creativity. Each student's unique cultural heritage and experiences contribute to a vibrant tapestry of knowledge that enhances research quality and fosters collaboration. Embracing this diversity allows scholars to engage in meaningful dialogue, challenge assumptions, and expand their horizons, ultimately leading to groundbreaking discoveries and advancements in their respective fields.

As international research students navigate their academic journeys, they encounter a wealth of opportunities to learn from one another. Engaging with diverse viewpoints can spark new ideas and inspire collaborative projects that transcend borders. By actively participating in discussions, workshops, and seminars, scholars can harness the collective intelligence of their peers, pushing the boundaries of traditional research. This collaborative spirit is essential for solving complex global issues, as it encourages interdisciplinary approaches and fosters an environment where innovative solutions can flourish.

Notes on Cultivating Resilience

Resilience is the ability to recover and adapt in the face of challenges.

Resilience, in the context of international research students, is the ability to **adapt, persevere, and thrive** in the face of academic, cultural, and personal challenges. It is not just about endurance but about growth—developing the capacity to navigate unfamiliar academic landscapes, overcome self-doubt, and transform obstacles into learning opportunities.

For those pursuing research in a new country, resilience means:

- **Intellectual adaptability**—grappling with new methodologies, expectations, and ways of thinking.
- **Emotional strength**—managing isolation, imposter syndrome, and the pressures of high-level study.
- **Cultural fluidity**—embracing new environments while holding onto one's identity.
- **Confidence in uncertainty**—seeing setbacks not as failures but as steps toward deeper understanding.

At *The Scholars' Mentor*, resilience is not just about surviving the journey but about **finding meaning, confidence, and a voice within it**.

Today, we explore how to build and nurture this important quality.

It is important to create a life you love, balancing relaxation with work

Exercise

1. Reflect on a moment in your academic or personal life when you overcame a difficult situation. Write about what happened and how you handled it.

2. Identify three qualities or skills that helped you in that situation (e.g., patience, creativity, perseverance).

3. Think about a current challenge you are facing. Write down one way that you can apply these qualities or skills to address it.

4. End by visualising yourself successfully overcoming this challenge, feeling stronger and more capable as a result.

Reflection

How did reflecting on past resilience help you feel more prepared to face current challenges?

Building Your Support Network

No journey is meant to be travelled alone. Today, we focus on identifying and strengthening your support network, both personally and professionally.

Exercise

1. Write down the names of five people who support you in your academic or personal life. These could be mentors, peers, friends, or family.

2. Next to each name, describe how they support you (e.g., offering advice, providing encouragement, helping with practical tasks).

3. Think of one way you can strengthen your relationship with each person. Write down a specific action (e.g., sending a thank-you note or scheduling a check-in call).

4. Finally, reflect on how you can offer support to others in your network. Write one way you can give back.

Reflection

What did you learn about your support system through this exercise? How can you nurture these connections further?

Dealing with Difficult People

We all encounter difficult people in our academic or personal lives, and even academic supervisors and peers can be super difficult people. Still, these challenges can be opportunities for growth. Today, we focus on using empathy and reframing their actions as tools for your own empowerment.

Exercise

1. Think about a person who has been difficult for you or perceived as very difficult for you), such as a supervisor, peer, or authority figure.

2.

2. Close your eyes and imagine their perspective. What pressures or challenges might they be facing? Write down your thoughts.

3. Reflect on how their behaviour could be teaching you something valuable. For example, is it helping you build resilience or clarity in your communication?

4. Write about one way you can approach them differently, using empathy as a tool. This could be a change in your mindset or a specific action.

Reflection

How did this exercise shift your perception of this person? What action will you take to empower yourself in this situation?

Creating Healthy Boundaries

Healthy boundaries are essential for maintaining balance and protecting your energy. Today, we reflect on how to set boundaries that support your well-being.

Exercise

1. Write down an area in your life where you feel your boundaries are being challenged (e.g., time, communication, or responsibilities).

2. Reflect on how this affects you—mentally, emotionally, or physically. Write about how stronger boundaries could improve your experience.

3. Create a script for how you could communicate this boundary respectfully. For example: 'I need to dedicate more time to my research, so I will not be available for [specific activity].'

4. Write one step you will take this week to establish or reinforce this boundary.

Reflection

How does setting boundaries make you feel? What do you notice about the balance it brings to your life?

Chapter 5

LEARN AGAIN: Strategies for International Research Students to Cope with Depression, Homesickness, and Low Mood

Introduction

At the beginning of this volume, I quoted from one of the rare articles which addresses international students head on. Just to remind you, here is what it said:

The article, titled *"The Experience of Loneliness Among International Students Participating in the BBC Loneliness Experiment"* (2023), analyses the experiences of loneliness among 521 international students aged 16–40 years. These participants were part of the BBC Loneliness Experiment, the largest international survey on loneliness to date. The study identifies the adverse social and psychological effects of loneliness on international students, emphasising its impact on emotional health, social functioning, and academic experiences.

Key Findings:

1. **Six Main Themes of Loneliness:**

   o **Negative Psychological and Social Aspects:** Feelings of emotional distress, social confusion, and diminished self-worth.

   o **Distressing Experience of Being Alone:** Isolation was perceived both subjectively and objectively, with students experiencing loneliness even in the presence of others.

   o **Disrupted Ability to Form Connections:** Language barriers, cultural differences, and lack of authentic connections made it difficult for students to integrate socially.

   o **Entrapment in Loneliness:** A sense of powerlessness and nihilism, with many reporting they felt unable to change their circumstances.

   o **Awareness of Stigma:** Many participants experienced self-stigma or fear of judgment, making them reluctant to admit their loneliness.

- **Positive Perceptions:**

A minority noted that loneliness could foster self-reflection or personal growth.

2. **Loneliness as a Prevalent Issue:**
   - Among the 521 students studied, 96% reported experiencing loneliness, with moderate to high-intensity levels in most cases. Students felt disconnected from family, friends, and local social circles.
   - Homesickness, discrimination, and perceived xenophobia compounded loneliness.

3. **Policy and Institutional Implications:**
   - The article emphasises the need for higher education institutions (HEIs) to address loneliness by promoting cross-cultural integration, providing mental health support, and creating opportunities for meaningful social interactions.
   - It advocates for training staff in inclusive teaching practices, buddy systems, and programs encouraging cultural exchange.

4. **Suggestions for Improvement:**
   - Institutions should prioritise initiatives that integrate international students with local students and address cultural and linguistic barriers.

- Digital tools and interventions targeting maladaptive social cognition may help reduce loneliness.

This study provides one of the most extensive qualitative analyses of international students' loneliness experiences, offering rich, descriptive data to inform policy and practice.

Highlighting the complex interplay of social, cultural, and psychological factors in shaping students' experiences of isolation and offering actionable recommendations to mitigate these challenges. The issues which we are addressing here are real, and yes, institutions and society could definitely do more to help, but meanwhile, the strategies offered in this volume can support your well-being.

As society continues to globalise, a growing number of international students contribute significantly to intellectual and cultural assets in a foreign academic setting, including the UK. Having ties with international academics fosters cross-cultural communication and enhances networks. The number of international research students, also known as research postgraduates, studying in UK universities has increased significantly in recent years. Research indicates that international research students experience various emotional challenges such as anxiety, low mood, feeling lost, culture shock, stress, and overthinking. This suggests a need to introduce creative and effective coping strategies that could help international research students release depressive symptoms during their study period.

It is crucial to note, however, that non-UK research students participating in a UK study cope with homesickness through dependency on technology, reaching out to family members or friends, and seeking social support. International students miss their families, food, people, and the climate. Deciding factors for missing home are depression, anger, loneliness, and separation from country, family, and school workers. Homesickness can lead to negative changes in mood, digestion, appetite, and other psychological matters. Even though universities in the UK provide some support, international students feel that their emotional needs are seldom addressed. Besides the concern about academic uncertainty, international students also have to face challenges pertaining to culture. As international students, they need to cope with a culture they are not familiar with and adapt quickly. Combining this with stress, dealing with educational and financial needs, and attempting to fit in could then compromise the international students' emotional well-being. Therefore, coping strategies in the context of culture are also highlighted in order to familiarise the students with solutions in times of anger, depression, shame, etc. The objectives of this paper are to help students find creative ways to release their personal depressive symptoms or assist in the coping process.

Prevalence of Depression, Homesickness, and Low Mood

You will forgive me for revisiting this article but it is vital as it gives solid academic basis for our discussions. Research has consistently found that international students experience mental health problems, such as depression, more frequently compared to domestic students. However, several studies have also shown that students in postgraduate courses are particularly vulnerable. The staggering statistic is that 38.8% of international research students met the threshold for a diagnosis of major depressive disorder. Still, high rates of homesickness were also found, with 67.8% having experienced high levels of homesickness.

Homesickness often precedes feelings of low mood before migration, which are more likely to continue to develop into full symptoms of depression post-migration.

Thus, this clearly represents a severe pre-existing problem for this group. In a recent study, it was reported that 14.6–34.2% of international research students met the diagnostic threshold for major depressive disorder from pre-arrival through to the end of the first year post-migration, indicating that symptom severity increased upon arrival in the host country. Whether these were new cases of depression or individuals already experiencing symptoms pre-migration is unclear from the study. Still, together, these findings underscore the seriousness of widespread homesickness in this population and suggest that post-migration, international research students may not only continue to experience homesickness but may also develop more severe and enduring difficulties such as low mood and/or depression.

Given the seriousness and frequency of pre-existing homesickness, feelings of low mood, and depression in this population, it is of paramount importance that robust exploration of these characteristics is cautious and can guide adequate support on a systematic basis. A targeted approach is notably critical for the international research student population due to their unique vulnerabilities, and ultimately, aiming to support this group is crucial to achieving success in academia overall. Screening on a regular basis and providing university, college, and external counselling support, specialist language and intercultural communication support, family and friendship support, or immigration advice and self-help strategies must be prioritised.

Effective Coping Strategies for Managing Low Mood and Preventing Depression

In this journey, it's important to focus on your mental well-being and adopt strategies that keep you resilient and thriving. Prevention is always better than seeking a cure when things become overwhelming. As an international research student, you face unique challenges, but by taking proactive steps to break down barriers and foster resilience, you can set yourself up for success. Let's explore some approaches to help you along the way.

Understanding Cultural Influences on Coping

Your cultural background often shapes your thoughts and coping mechanisms. For example, if you come from an individualistic culture, you might value personal achievement over social connections, which can sometimes lead to feelings of isolation. On the other hand, if you're from a collectivist culture, you may place a higher value on family, social networks, or authority figures for support, but you might also feel a stigma about seeking life coaching and even formal counselling.

If you're worried about how seeking counselling might be perceived, first consider a life coach, but at some times, only a counsellor or a therapist might be suitable. Take a moment to reflect on this with a counsellor or trusted person who can provide an objective view. A counsellor can help you weigh the pros and cons and explore what's best for your well-being. Later in this book, I'll share more about what to expect in counselling so you can make an informed decision if that's a path you'd like to consider.

Developing Your Coping Skills

Throughout this book, we have looked together at different aspects of your mental health in a host country. Here again, I want to stress that it is your responsibility to make sure your well-being is well catered for – it is essential to grab signals for your low mood and unhappiness when it is still easy to resolve this. We will be looking at different kinds of meditation, which, alongside regular exercise, will help you find the strength to go out to the world and make new physical connections.

While your advisor or family may provide support, your personal power base comes from how you care for yourself. This means developing coping skills that you can rely on, even when things feel beyond your control. A strong support network will also help you discover and practice new ways to cope with challenges.

Embracing Self-Care

Make self-care a priority. Use the recreational facilities available to you. Regular exercise, whether it's sports, walking, or another activity you enjoy, is a great way to elevate your mood and release pent-up feelings like frustration or anger. Physical activity is not just good for your body—it's a boost for your mind, too.

Seeking Professional Help

Remember, asking for help is a sign of strength, not weakness. If you notice signs like persistent low mood or thoughts of self-harm, reach out for professional support. Early intervention can make a big difference, and there's no shame in seeking guidance from advisors or mental health professionals.

By taking these steps, you're not just coping—you're building the tools to thrive in your academic and personal life.

Building Your Support Network: Practical Tips for Feeling Less Alone

Feeling lonely is a common challenge, especially when you're navigating the demands of research. It's also one of the early signs of mental health struggles. But remember, you don't have to face this alone. Building a support network can not only provide practical help—like a hand with errands or a listening ear—but also remind you that you're not the only one feeling this way. Here's how you can start creating meaningful connections:

Overcoming Shyness and Starting Conversations

Making the first move can feel daunting, but it's a skill you can develop. Start small: when you're in a shared space, like the library or a common area, smile and say hello to someone nearby. These small interactions often lead to deeper conversations over time. For example, if you notice someone working on a similar topic or using the same resources, ask them a question—it's a great way to break the ice.

If you feel anxious about initiating contact, remind yourself that others may feel the same way. Many students are eager to make friends but might be unsure of how to start. Taking that first step can create a positive connection for both of you.

Using Your Environment to Meet People

The library isn't just for books—it's also a great space to connect with other students. Study groups are a particularly effective way to meet people who share your academic interests and improve your productivity. If one doesn't already exist, consider starting your own.

Conferences and symposia are excellent for building professional networks, though they can feel intimidating at first. Start small: prepare a couple of questions you'd like to ask during discussions. After sessions, approach someone whose perspective interested you and introduce yourself. Networking at these events gets easier with practice, and every small interaction helps.

Joining Clubs, Sports, and Professional Groups

Clubs and societies are fantastic for connecting with like-minded people. Whether you join a professional association, a cultural society, or a hobby group, these settings provide a relaxed environment to share experiences and learn from your peers. Student services or campus notice boards are great places to find opportunities.

Sports clubs, in particular, can be an excellent way to combine physical activity with socialising. Consider joining a running club, a football or volleyball team, or even a dance class. Many universities offer recreational classes like yoga, Zumba, or salsa dancing—these are not only fun and energising but also fantastic for meeting others who share your interests. Physical activities release endorphins, boosting your mental health while creating connections in an informal and enjoyable setting.

Social Media and Online Communities

Social media can be a powerful tool for finding and engaging with communities. Platforms like LinkedIn or academic forums often host groups for researchers in your field, while Facebook or WhatsApp groups might connect you with students at your university. Seek out spaces that feel positive and inclusive, where you can share experiences, ask questions, and find support.

Always use social media responsibly. Focus on fostering genuine connections rather than comparing yourself to others. Many platforms also host communities for shared interests, like running, dancing, or cultural groups, so you can find networks that resonate with you.

Being Sensitive to Cultural Differences

As you engage with others, it's important to stay mindful of cultural differences. Not everyone may feel comfortable with activities that involve alcohol or certain cultural practices. Look for inclusive events and meet-ups that welcome people from all backgrounds and create an environment where everyone feels valued.

Sharing Your Experiences

Sharing your personal story can be a powerful way to connect with others. Whether it's in a peer support group, a social media post, or a small gathering, being open about your experiences often resonates with others who feel the same way. It might even lead to opportunities to share your story with wider audiences, helping to normalise these feelings and inspire others.

Building a support network might feel challenging at first, but every small step you take—whether it's joining a club, starting a conversation, or attending an event—will bring you closer to creating a community that uplifts and supports you. Along the way, you'll find that the connections you make not only ease your loneliness but also enrich your academic and personal journey.

Embracing Self-Care: A Gentle Gift to Yourself

Self-care is more than a buzzword; it's an act of kindness toward yourself—a way to pause, breathe, and remind yourself that you are worthy of care and attention. In the whirlwind of research deadlines, personal expectations, and the constant push for achievement, it's easy to put yourself last. But self-care is not selfish—it's the foundation of your well-being. Think of it as planting seeds that will grow into resilience, focus, and joy. Each small step you take to care for yourself adds colour and depth to the picture of your life, making it not just about work and responsibilities but about balance and fulfilment.

Self-care isn't always about grand gestures or time-intensive routines. Sometimes, it's the little things—a few moments of calm, a deliberate choice to nourish your body, or allowing yourself the space to truly relax—that can make the biggest difference. Let's explore how you can gently weave self-care into your daily life and begin to feel its uplifting effects.

What Does Self-Care Look Like for You?

Before we dive into suggestions, take a moment to reflect: What does self-care mean to you? Is it taking a break to enjoy your favourite music, stepping outside to feel the sun on your face, or indulging in a creative hobby that brings you joy? Self-care is deeply personal, and there's no right or wrong way to approach it. The key is finding practices that help you feel balanced, rejuvenated, and connected to yourself.

Finding Joy in the Simple Moments

Start small and simple. Have you ever considered the magic of a warm bath? Light a candle, play some soothing music, and let the water wash away the stress of your day. It's not just about relaxation—it's about creating a moment that's entirely yours, a space where you can let go and simply be.

If you enjoy arts or culture, why not treat yourself to a theatre performance or a film? Better yet, invite a friend along. Sharing these experiences not only enhances your enjoyment but also deepens your connections with others. If that's not your style, perhaps a quiet evening reading a book or sketching your thoughts can be just as rewarding.

Recreation and Hobbies: A Gateway to Balance

Recreation is a wonderful way to step outside the pressures of daily life. Think about hobbies or activities that bring you joy. What sparks your interest? It might be gardening, baking, writing, or even something adventurous like joining a local dance class. If you're not sure where to start, think back to activities you loved as a child or try something completely new. Many universities offer workshops or clubs for interests like photography, pottery, or even board games. These not only help you unwind but can also lead to meeting others with shared passions.

For physical activities, you might find joy in a running group, a yoga class, or even a casual game of volleyball.

Movement is a powerful mood booster, and the camaraderie of group activities can ease feelings of loneliness. Remember, self-care is about what feels good to you, so experiment until you find your fit.

Graduation and joyful celebrations with my postgraduate students in 2019

Prioritising Nutrition and Sleep

Your body works hard to support you, and it deserves care in return. Eating a balanced diet isn't just about fuelling your body—it's about honouring it. Try incorporating colourful fruits, vegetables, and whole grains into your meals. Even something as simple as cooking with a friend can transform the mundane into a moment of connection and creativity.

Sleep, too, is a cornerstone of self-care. If you've been skimping on rest, it's time to prioritise it. Create a bedtime routine that signals to your body it's time to wind down. Put away your devices, dim the lights, and perhaps read or listen to calming music before bed. You'll be amazed at how much better you feel after a good night's sleep.

Setting Boundaries with Work

In the academic world, there's often an unspoken expectation to work tirelessly. But burnout is real, and ignoring your own needs will only make it harder to succeed. Give yourself permission to set boundaries. Schedule regular breaks during your day—these might be as short as a few minutes to stretch or breathe deeply. Apps like Headspace or Calm can guide you through quick mindfulness exercises or provide ideas for movement breaks.

Beyond the workday, make sure you also set aside time for activities that bring you joy and mental stimulation. Whether it's reading for pleasure, exploring a hobby, or connecting with friends, these moments of balance will help you return to your studies with renewed energy and focus.

Try Something Today: A Gentle Experiment

What could you do today to care for yourself? Maybe it's stepping outside for a short walk, preparing a healthy meal, or trying a simple relaxation exercise. If you're feeling adventurous, explore a new hobby or join a local club. Keep in mind that self-care is a journey. You don't have to overhaul your routine overnight. Instead, choose one or two practices to try and notice how they make you feel. Over time, these small acts of kindness toward yourself can create lasting change.

A Reminder to Be Kind to Yourself

You deserve to feel good. You deserve to take up space, to rest, and to thrive. Self-care is a way to remind yourself of your worth and to cultivate the resilience you need to navigate the demands of life as a research student. Each small step is a step toward balance and well-being. Start today—you're worth it.

Seeking Professional Help

In the introduction to this volume, I mentioned how, at the onset of my own doctoral journey, I experienced feelings of anxiety and discouragement. I was fairly close to dropping out. I remember walking around Bloomsbury, thinking, 'All these wonderful women were hanging out here as part of the Bloomsbury set, like Virginia Woolf and Vita Sackville-West, creating a memorable legacy, and here I am having doubts about my own research journey.' I did seek help fairly early in my PhD journey, and I did find it very helpful. However, in hindsight, too much focus was paid to my childhood and not enough to the challenges at hand. I kept going through and succeeded, and even got the College prize for getting my doctorate with no corrections. What I did not say in the introduction is that this was not my first go at doing a PhD; I did start a DPhil at Oxford 18 years previously, and I did drop out in the first semester – it was too bizarre, too English and too hostile. Almost 2 decades after that experience, and after so many successes in my personal and professional life, yet again, I felt terrible, but this time, I sought help and stayed the course.

Often, there is a tendency to 'harden up' and not ask for help instead of seeing that asking for assistance is an action in self-management. National and some local mental health services will often provide some resource information on how to deal with distressing emotions with mild to moderate self-help guides. University counselling services and mental health advisory teams offer you the opportunity to speak freely and openly in a relaxed, one-on-one environment. As an international research student, you might face moments of isolation or emotional challenges without realising that a range of supportive services is available to help you. However, if you feel uncomfortable asking for help from the host university, turn to other life coaching opportunities, including, of course, the Scholars' Mentor.

By engaging with these resources, you can better understand the difficulties you're facing and begin developing strategies to enhance your mental well-being. Often, these strategies focus on preventing challenges from escalating rather than simply treating symptoms. Taking the step to connect with these services could be a turning point in your journey to both personal and academic success.

Cultural Considerations and Coping Mechanisms

We have already established that the cultural background of international research students is of importance. It also plays a crucial role in determining their willingness to seek help as well as coping strategies.

At times, as a result of mental illness stigma, students are less likely to access mental health services. Help-seeking barriers for international research students could include that people from Eastern cultures fear losing face or shame themselves and their families should they access mental health services, or that people from collectivist cultures may fear gossip in close-knit communities when seeking help.

Cultures and societies have coping mechanisms at the broad community, societal, and individual levels. From a cultural perspective, mental well-being could be influenced by various rituals and traditions. Learning from and integrating these natural coping mechanisms into educational research is key to developing effective support frameworks.

For example, certain cultures and traditions have demonstrated lower prevalence rates of depression compared to others, and perhaps there is something to be learnt here. Extended families and close communities help reduce social isolation and feelings of emotional distress, which both contribute to the development of depressive symptoms. Research suggests that culture-specific healing rituals and ceremonies might be beneficial in reducing depression in developing countries. It is vital to train mental health practitioners to be attuned to the helping process evident in these cultural self-help groups and to place value in indigenous healing methods.

Cultural Differences in Mental Health Stigma

As an international research student, you might face unique challenges when it comes to mental health. Cultural differences can shape the way you experience and address mental health issues. Your views on mental health resources may vary depending on where you're from, and it's not uncommon to feel like you're held to higher standards in managing your mental well-being.

Your background, customs, and cultural values all play a role in how you handle mental health challenges. For example, in places like Australia or the USA, people often prioritise mental health and encourage open conversations about it. But if you're from countries like China, India, Japan, Spain, Saudi Arabia, or Austria, you might find that mental health is approached differently. Talking about your struggles openly, seeking support from friends or family, or even considering professional help may not feel natural—or even acceptable—in the way you're used to.

When you come to study abroad, these cultural stigmas can follow you. You might feel torn between two worlds: trying to adapt to your new environment while also holding onto the cultural norms you grew up with. Here, you may face shame, isolation, or a sense of struggle while worrying about how acknowledging your mental health challenges could affect your family or reputation back home.

The good news is that there are ways to make mental health more approachable for you and your peers. Workshops, educational programs, therapy sessions, and even community initiatives can create safe spaces for you to talk about mental health without judgment. It's not just about destigmatising mental illness—it's about normalising conversations around emotional well-being. You can start by participating in open dialogues, where you and others define what mental health and emotional wellness mean to you.

Imagine having opportunities to discuss these topics with fellow students, professors, and mentors. By taking part in these conversations, you could be part of a movement that fosters emotional intelligence and supports others like you. Together, you can create a culture of understanding and openness where seeking help is seen as a strength, not a weakness.

You also have the power to lead these initiatives. Whether it's brainstorming new strategies for wellness programs or organising events to promote awareness, you can help shape a supportive environment on campus.

When everyone works together—students, faculty, and staff—you can make it easier for others to feel comfortable seeking help and overcoming the stigma around mental health.

By engaging with emotional well-being, you'll not only help yourself but also inspire others to do the same. The more open you are to understanding and addressing mental health, the more at ease you'll feel—and the more empowered you'll be in every aspect of your life. You're not alone in this journey, and together, we can create a world where mental health is valued, understood, and supported.

Cultural Practices that Promote Mental Well-Being

Previous studies have found the role of tradition and social customs in preventing and reducing symptoms of mental illness. For example, Latino caregivers participate in the custom of Velorio, in which they come together in the event of death to sing and provide support for each other. Participation in Velorio was associated with lower symptoms of trauma. 'Gemenos,' in Greek culture, are communal gatherings of people who support each other in times of grief. In Arab culture, families come together, especially during events such as a 'Hafli' or during

Ramadan, in order to help cope with the heartache of missing family members at significant times. Arab and Pakistani families tend to come together on weekends and celebrate special dinners with singing, clapping, laughter, and joy to take away loneliness during special times. These practices foster resilience to depression through the giving and receiving of social support. Mental health counselling would value incorporating these traditions and cultural practices.

Mental health challenges

Overall, the fact is that loneliness and isolation were exacerbated by several difficulties, such as not being able to communicate effectively in English, work-related stress, cultural shock, and experiences in Western societies that are received negatively. Consequently, the most adopted strategies to cope with depression, homesickness, and low mood were building a social network, using the Internet to speak with family and friends in their own countries of origin, and engaging in self-care practices. Because participants' strategies reflect some proactive coping strategies, the main implication is that feeling supported would contribute to their well-being. Also, mindfulness and meditative practices have been shown to increase well-being and a sense of calm and purpose.

Future research should engage in a longitudinal study on international research students, which may investigate the change in the prevalence of depression and changes in coping style and degree of homesickness from the time of arrival to the completion of their studies. Moreover, a cross-cultural study on international students' mental health in terms of different socio-cultural contexts for Australasian, Western European, and US/Canadian groups may also be beneficial to improve understanding of the context of depression in international research students in varied national settings. Further research could focus on interventions using randomised controlled trials with various sample sectors, such as international students, exchange students, or vacation students, and evaluate the effectiveness of workplace-based education and training around depression and how to respond to symptoms of depression. Moreover, the effectiveness of intervention programs, such as buddy programs in schools or tertiary institutions, designed to support students and decrease loneliness or homesickness, could also be researched.

There is widespread professional interest in how mental health can be improved for international students, including research into the sorts of interventions and support services that are likely to be particularly beneficial. Universities are increasingly collaborating with mental health professionals in ways that may either implicitly or explicitly reduce a student's readiness and access to external help from a professional mental health service when they need it. Future research that aims to track the broader context of how educational institutions deal with mental health issues in the student population may require a research methodology that collaborates with both academic institutions and mental health professionals over time. In this endeavour, it will be essential to understand how international students and local students are differently implicated in various allied entry-to-practice policies and professional disciplinary bodies in the field of mental health policy and service provisions.

Empathy

Some of the strategies suggested may take a long time and, for some cultures and individual personalities, are very difficult to achieve, impact the person's authenticity, and may actually be seen as a personal rejection of the person who is being rejected or denigrated. As such, empathy must be considered as one tool available to people in responding to these situations.

A conversation about the importance of empathy as a tool to help us live better is long overdue. International research students might be able to cope with unwanted feelings of denigration and rejection.

Understanding Rejection and Denigration

Denigration is defined derogatively as a denial of approval, e.g., a communication showing that one's work or something about oneself is disrespectful or has shortcomings. One can further distinguish between social denigration and professional denigration. Rejection is defined as a withdrawal of approval, sometimes also accompanied by a wish that one had never tried or shown up. They are believed to be prevalent in academic settings, with social isolation and negative social feedback found to be common experiences among international research students. International research students may also experience an absence of support, which can manifest in unsupportive supervision.

International research students often find their academic learning curves and social experiences with Western education fall short of their expectations or ideals. Rejection and denigration sometimes lead to feelings of depression, although we found no evidence of the causes, either precipitating or perpetuating depression due to denigration for international research students. Feelings of anger and aggressiveness are reported as direct responses to denigration in the professional domain. The emotional and psychological toll of being rejected and denigrated can be significant, leaving individuals less likely to think and behave in ways that are congruent with their current or desired perceptual goals. When rejected, individuals tend to permit themselves to express internally motivated behaviour, even if it is unusual or novel, i.e., to let the pendulum of self-expression swing toward the unfamiliar. Conversely, when one feels denigrated, they often return to what they are comfortable and familiar with; rather than feeling inclined to improve, people work to demonstrate their perceived competency in the domain in which they have been denigrated.

Types of Rejection and Denigration in Academic Settings

It is necessary to note that rejection and denigration potentially involve several typologies. For instance, peer rejection in informal settings or in the context of group work was reported to be an uncomfortable experience. Such occurrences can denote a lack of ability to socially integrate or can make it difficult to mix with fellow students, which makes academic environments an unfriendly place to be. An emphasis on peer efforts and interdependence can help limit exclusionary economic behaviour. More diminished forms of relationships are still relative to the institutional settings, though, such as a lack of sympathetic personnel available to guide home and international students in developing their academic literacy. This frugality impacts performance.

Types of interpersonal rejection may include not acknowledging or avoiding another person, purposefully excluding them from interactions, and being overly unaccepting, prejudiced, or uncivil. It is possible that, at times, the perceived rejection is culturally determined. That is to say, the 'author' of the rejection did not mean to be rude but was a little impersonal. At other times, of course, there is evidence for these rejections.

Interpersonally, denial ranges from the serious, such as people rejecting another's application for a specific role, to the mild, such as actively avoiding colleagues with whom one has had a disagreement. However, they have not necessarily been a "bad" person. Being involved in too much of what another person says or does is another indication of not accepting another, which casts them into a role of purposeful denial. While some thought rejection was rare, identification of scenarios of being led to feel judged by something had no relation to demography or repatriation and occurred predominantly from student sources. This involved what was felt by the students, the language testers, and the employers. Inappropriate judgment of the students' language knowledge base made them feel that they, as people, were being sized up in a self-destructive way. They internalised rejection from others and questioned their self-worth or doubted their ability. Such emotional harm was not limited just to international students and is an indicator of the emotional dimensions of human bonding and fundamental human needs, as well as being a contributor to academic exclusivity. International students have expressed that they are not sure their needs are being catered to by staff that they are to feel they belong in this culture. Some research students have been disgruntled by the unfairness of ethnic international students springing ahead of them in terms of skill knowledge and understanding, yet being unable to get their message across as skillfully, especially when they know the text is to have an original and contrived spin on an old issue—quotas for admission help to acknowledge the existence of a set of barriers between the interlocutor and you. Structures of narrow awareness of the barriers stemming from educational ignorance regarding the implications of intercultural communication need to be addressed.

The Role of Empathy in Coping Strategies

Empathy is the ability to step beyond oneself and truly inhabit the perspective of another. It is not merely recognising another person's emotions but deeply understanding their experience—intellectually, emotionally, and even ethically.

Philosophically, empathy bridges the gap between **self and other**, reminding us that knowledge and connection are relational. Thinkers like **Edith Stein** and **Martha Nussbaum** emphasise that empathy is not passive sympathy; it is an active, transformative engagement with another's reality.

For international researchers, empathy is essential—it allows us to navigate new cultural landscapes, embrace diverse perspectives, and foster meaningful academic and human connections.

Empathy can be a powerful tool to help you navigate rejections, criticism, and stress. Instead of letting societal, academic, or personal doubts weigh you down, try to approach these challenges with understanding—both for yourself and for others. Empathy allows you to build resilience by seeing actions and emotions in a new light.

When you develop empathy, you're not just strengthening your relationships with others—you're also cultivating a healthier relationship with yourself. It helps you stay true to your values, cope with flaws and obstacles, and feel a sense of shared humanity. Empathy reminds you that you're not alone and can even deepen your sense of fairness and justice for yourself and those around you.

On a larger scale, empathy can bring people together. By fostering a sense of community and mutual support, you can help create an academic environment where everyone feels valued. When students from different backgrounds—whether from the global North or South—connect through understanding, it helps prevent misunderstandings and discrimination. Empathy bridges the gaps, encouraging cooperation and mutual respect.

You can start by validating your own feelings and those of others. Acknowledge your emotions, share your struggles, and listen with an open heart. In doing so, you'll contribute to a supportive learning environment where everyone can thrive. And when it comes to bigger challenges, like addressing racism or other forms of discrimination, empathy can be a cornerstone for meaningful conversations and collective healing.

It is important to clarify that we encourage a multidimensional understanding of empathy that stretches from an awareness of one's own emotional landscape, reactions, and embodied experiences to the support for others' needs and values and respect that underlies many forms of social relations. While empathy is commonly regarded as a means of extending one's understanding of others' contexts, it is also beneficial to take an empathic perspective towards oneself. In order to grow empathy, a series of shared activities exist. These exercises encompass active listening as if perspective-taking, role-playing, imagining oneself in someone else's place, discussing their viewpoints, and participating in a creative act to describe the thoughts, feelings, and behaviors of other people. In difficult moments, cultivating an empathic approach might, if used actively, work as a friend, a mentor, and an anchor.

Challenges of Deploying Empathy

It is crucial to ponder whether empathy should extend even when faced with rejection and denigration in the academic realm. International students pursuing postgraduate research are often perceived by others, as well as by themselves, as early career academics. Thus, this argument will rest on the premise that international students resemble early-career staff in training, dedicating time and effort to establishing themselves as recognised and respected professionals in their respective fields. Considering that research often intertwines with personal identity and self-worth, particularly regarding the differentiation between individuals deemed sufficiently intellectual and creative (who identify themselves as individuals of value) and those who are not, empathy assumes paramount importance in this context. Both international students, who aspire for their research to be acknowledged as commendable and labour-intensive, and the necessity for them to possess attributes such as 'good problem-solving' skills, find themselves directly confronting denigration and rejection. Such encounters can be all-consuming, as they undermine the integrity of their self-identity.

Empathy is a point on which both psychological and neurological science and the psychological backing of philosophical work agree. The skills of empathy— cognitive empathy as the understanding of another's viewpoint, perspective, and mindscape; affective empathy as being able to share another's internal emotional states with an appropriate emotional response—are developed as a part of what has allowed the human species to form intricate social networks offering support, companionship, and cooperative endeavours. This is crucial for the student experience—it builds and fosters a strong sense of normality and can allow for the breakthrough, so to speak, into new personal and interpersonal abilities that would not have occurred without a little bit of deep cognitive work about relationships (a sub-part of cognitive empathy) that involved a lot of precursors about who and how we as researchers, international students, and people.

The skills of empathy—cognitive empathy as the profound understanding of another person's viewpoint, perspective, and mindscape; affective empathy as being able to genuinely share another individual's internal emotional states with an appropriate emotional response—are developed as a part of what has allowed the human species to form intricate and interconnected social networks that offer profound support, companionship, and cooperative endeavours. This is of utmost importance for the student experience—it builds and nurtures a remarkably strong and unwavering sense of normality and can allow for an extraordinary breakthrough, so to speak, into new and uncharted personal and interpersonal abilities that would not have come to fruition without delving deep into cognitive work about relationships (which is a vital sub-part of cognitive empathy) and undertaking a multitude of precursors regarding who we are, how we function as researchers, international students, and individuals in this complex world. Nevertheless, the true extent of the impact that facilitating those empathetic links will actually achieve remains somewhat unclear, and it may not even be the most advantageous form of inquiry into the subject. In fact, it is plausible to hypothesise that deep cognitive empathy not only effectively 'facilitates' intricate networks of relation, but this very development, harmoniously, genuinely engenders the act of introducing other individuals into entirely fresh and unexplored relations (such as critical and positive thinking, for instance), thus enabling us to forge the very tools that empower us to resist various challenges and complexities existing in a particular context, be it at the national, local/international, research-based, epistemological, or theoretical level.

Practical Techniques for Cultivating Empathy

At times, it is better to deploy empathy to try to understand the other person's motivations and point of view instead of just feeling hurt or angry.

Empathy plays a critical role in addressing the challenges of denigration, exclusion, and rejection. Empathy can be used in many ways but also as an attempt to understand the point of view of the person who has hurt you – perhaps inadvertently. Perhaps they did try and be helpful – and failed. Nonetheless, it might be more helpful to you as a research student to understand that they are attempting to be helpful but are also human and might have had a bad day and expressed their assessments inappropriately. Empathy is different from forgiveness, although forgiveness might follow. Empathy allows you to understand and learn and become empowered. That is why it is important.

Developing self-awareness, particularly through empathetic understanding, helps not only to process personal experiences of rejection but also to foster resilience. It also aids professionals in navigating complex interpersonal and ethical dilemmas with emotional intelligence. Cultivating empathy requires us to move beyond harbouring anger or resentment for past rejections. Instead, it involves engaging in practices that encourage understanding and connection.

One practical method to develop empathy is through collaborative learning workshops. In such settings, rejected materials could become case studies, allowing participants to practice non-judgmental listening, collaborative mentoring, and facilitation skills. These workshops serve as a platform for enhancing the empathetic capacity of joint supervision teams working with international research students.

Active listening is another cornerstone of empathy-building. Conflict resolution workshops provide an opportunity to hone this skill, emphasising the importance of listening without judgment. As graduate educators, developing empathetic listening skills enables us to build more adaptive relationships and negotiate fair and equitable power dynamics in day-to-day researcher-supervisor interactions.

Empathy is also closely tied to fostering a sense of community. For instance, co-authoring workshops could incorporate empathy-building exercises. One example is a behavioural activity where participants identify their colleagues' personal strengths, burdens, and milestones, culminating in a celebration that reflects the group's shared experiences. This design-thinking approach not only supports personal resilience but also lays the groundwork for creating a more inclusive and empathetic environment for international students.

Imagine a professional environment where coaches and trainers excel in practical empathy-building techniques. By fostering these skills, we can create a supportive atmosphere that not only strengthens individual resilience but also cultivates a community where empathy thrives. Such an environment has the potential to transform how we approach education and mentorship for international research students.

Expanded Self-compassion and Self-Care Practices

Self-compassion has gained recent attention as a complementary practice to foster empathy in corporate settings. Described as a way of turning understanding and kindness inward, it is most notably defined by three core elements: kind, connected, and mindful attention to oneself when facing adversity from a broad perspective or to oneself as part of an imperfect human condition. It provides a construct of self-compassion based on six clear aspects: self-kindness (versus self-judgment), common humanity (versus isolation), mindfulness (versus over-identification), self-kindness (versus over-identification), common humanity (versus fierce rejection), and mindfulness (versus self-serving).

For international research students, self-compassion is presented as a way to reduce negative emotional and behavioural responses to rejection and denigration and to facilitate the resilience process against these adversities that newcomers face in both academic and personal contexts. Through kindness to oneself, rather than being cold and uninvolved with their suffering, the negative emotions and self-evaluations that arise while attempting to learn research life, self-care, and everything else from panel feedback become softer. Guidance for self-compassionate coping is also a push to treat oneself as someone you care about, as many researchers offer kindness and mindfulness practices such as common meditation techniques. Nurtured students and staff are usually enthusiastic about taking care of their colleagues and friends, which may become unhealthy at a great emotional cost. Energy and mood shifts seem possible.

Applying Empathy in Interactions with Supervisors: Cultivating Understanding and Trust in Managing Rejection and Uncertainties as an International Research Student

International research students and their supervisors report that the most critical concern for successful working relationships is effective communication. Below I list the general statements which are aspirational rather than actual – for a variety of reasons. It is here where a counsellor or a life coach could be deployed to support an international student when the supervisory arrangements do not allow for any support beyond the simple academic 'know-how.'

Naturally, one would hope that the institution would offer this support to international students, but they often do not. Leadership and motivation research with international students also highlight the need for the engagement of international postgraduate students, and strategies can be used to improve leader-member relationships. Communication can be used effectively to build these relationships through the engagement of others in appropriate dialogues. This successful dialogue uses an empathetic response, which signals to the other that a person fully understands their situation. This could be done through reflective listening and open-ended questions, which set an atmosphere for empathy and are not just problem-solving inquiries. The dialogue must be characterised by clarity and frankness, allowing a full understanding of the situation and the concern. Courteousness and respect should control the dialogue. How we deliver these messages is are indicator of the use of empathy. Clearly, in the current neo-liberal economic climate

This is especially important as the research has indicated that virtually all students generally appear to have common concerns in their academic supervision interactions; these concerns revolve around feeling isolated, difficulty in obtaining a quick and appropriate response, the quality of their relationship with their supervisor, and understandable and constructive feedback.

Despite these perceived concerns, it has been argued that there is a clear deficit in the literature in supporting the development of successful supervision interactions. Effective communication requires all academics to be able to engage in empathetic experiences, as they are regularly confronted with significant situations of distress and/or difficulties from their research students. When effectively used, dialogue can self-repair an ailing relationship, as understanding between supervisor and student can quickly be built. Barriers to students may be a lack of confidence, social skills, or cultural differences. Barriers for supervisors include a lack of rapport techniques, work pressure, and too many students' syndrome. Regardless of these factors, comprehensive literature, primary data, and anecdotal evidence strongly support the use of effective, empathetic engagement through effective, responsive dialogue to mend broken relationships. Practice of these skills can be carried out in activities such as role-play and using feedback loops.

Celebrating a success with one of my students

Mindfulness and Meditation Practices

Mindfulness and meditation practices offer a transformative approach for international research scholars navigating the complexities of academic life. As you immerse yourself in a new culture, the demands of your research can feel overwhelming. Mindfulness invites you to anchor yourself in the present moment, fostering a deeper connection to your surroundings and your inner self. This practice encourages you to observe your thoughts and feelings without judgment, creating a space for clarity and focus amid the challenges of academic pursuits. By incorporating mindfulness into your daily routine, you cultivate resilience and adaptability, essential qualities for thriving in a foreign environment.

Meditation, a key component of mindfulness, provides an opportunity to calm the mind and rejuvenate the spirit. Whether you choose to engage in guided meditation, breathing exercises, or silent reflection, dedicating time each day to this practice can significantly enhance your mental well-being. For international research scholars facing the pressures of deadlines, cultural adaptation, and the pursuit of excellence, meditation serves as a sanctuary. It allows you to step back from the whirlwind of responsibilities, enabling you to recharge and return to your work with renewed vigour and creativity.

Integrating mindfulness and meditation into your academic life not only aids in stress management but also enhances your overall performance. Research shows that regular mindfulness practice leads to improved concentration, better decision-making, and increased emotional intelligence. These qualities are particularly valuable for international scholars who must navigate diverse academic environments and build relationships across cultures. By honing your ability to remain present and engaged, you position yourself to seize opportunities and overcome obstacles with grace and confidence.

As you embark on your journey of mindfulness, consider the cultural dimensions that shape your experience. Each culture has its own practices and beliefs surrounding well-being and mental health. Embracing mindfulness allows you to blend traditional practices from your home culture with new techniques you encounter in your host country. This fusion not only enriches your personal practice but also fosters a sense of belonging and connection with both your roots and your new community. Your unique perspective can contribute to a more inclusive understanding of well-being among your peers, creating a supportive network where everyone thrives.

Ultimately, I see that mindfulness and meditation are not just practices but pathways to success for international research scholars. You can simply choose an element of these techniques and use it as one of many in your toolbox. This is not some kind of 'woo woo' approach – it is a time-honoured approach to give you peace and solace in times of stress.

They empower you to navigate the intricacies of academic life with a sense of purpose and balance. By committing to this journey, you cultivate a mindset that embraces challenges as opportunities for growth. As you learn to listen to your inner voice and honour your needs, you become an advocate for your own well-being, setting a powerful example for others. In the heart of your research journey, let mindfulness and meditation be your guides, illuminating the path to not only academic success but a fulfilling life experience.

The Benefits and Techniques of Meditation

1. Introduction to Meditation

Meditation is a practice that has been around for thousands of years and has been found in religious contexts as varied as Hinduism, Buddhism, and Judaism. In each of these traditions, meditation has been presented as a way to increase inner tranquillity, enhance self-awareness, and have a chance to rebuild the self that we present to the world. Its existence in so many cultures, often unrelated to one another, is one reason why many scientific researchers are now examining it for potential medical or psychological benefits. The purpose of meditation is to give people time apart from the hectic world, slow down busy thinking, and interact in a calming activity that encourages relaxation and a sense of peace. Many individuals in the medical and psychological industries have accepted it as an effective way to relieve stress and anxiety.

Meditation prevents the brain from being overwhelmed with distracting and unwelcome thoughts. Several current meditation types still involve deep thought and reflection on a variety of subjects, such as physical fitness, mental or spiritual wellness, or even plans for the future. There are also some very simple yet reliable methods. The efficacy and ease of these techniques have made meditation progressively popular and widely used for many purposes. It has become so normal in Western culture that various platforms have sprouted up in online and regional environments, enabling people to find out the best methods and ways for their conditions and needs. Meditation has become so famous worldwide that globally, most people use some form of self-reflection as part of their everyday life. For a more in-depth understanding of both the advantages of meditation and its various techniques, please proceed to the next sections.

The Physical and Mental Benefits of Meditation

There is an increasing body of evidence that substantiates the physical and mental health benefits associated with meditation. Scientific research demonstrates that regular meditation can decrease stress, lower blood pressure, decrease inflammation, and positively affect immune function. One study has found that individuals who meditated over the span of two months experienced as much as a 50% increase in antibody production compared to a control group. Alternatively, hands-on healing work or guided meditation may produce a deeper state of relaxation and dishabituation. Meditation has been shown to decrease symptoms of PTSD as well. This can, in turn, lower levels of perceived stress and other symptoms. As previously mentioned, decreased levels of stress can produce numerous physical health benefits. Meditation has been shown to significantly improve pain tolerance. During an EEG theta brain wave state, a person's pain threshold has been shown to increase.

Meditation increases focus, attention, and the ability to work under stress. In recent years, meditation has been the subject of controlled clinical research and has been found to have other effects. For example, it has been found to lower the symptoms of anxiety, depression, and ADHD.

It has also been observed to increase cortical thickness in areas that typically diminish with age. Regular meditation also aids in the proper regulation of emotions. Regulation of emotions may also help prevent short-term levels of stress from turning into chronic stress. Psychoneuroimmunology is the science that studies the increase or decrease of immune function as related to the mind. Meditation has been observed in many studies to increase immune function. Psychological and neuropsychological research has shown different types of meditation can affect the brain in different ways. The focus and attention-based practices have been termed 'focused attention' meditations, whereas the practices designed to increase a sense of compassion and further positive feelings and thoughts are termed 'open monitoring' meditations.

Different Meditation Techniques

In any form of meditation, the key to success lies in finding a technique that works for you and one that encourages you to continue. Here are some of the most common forms of meditation, all of which have specific traits designed to appeal to different types of people. Transcendental Meditation is big on mantras and the process of going into your mind and seeking out stress and tension, and replacing it with the peaceful action of transcending. The immediate positive effects: If you're really into the movement of transcending and are keen on searching for the causes of stress within, then give it a go. There are some courses which are a combination of yoga, meditation, and group processes. At the crux of the practice is a breathing technique that eliminates stress, fatigue, and negative emotions such as anger, frustration, and depression, leaving you calm yet energised, focused yet relaxed. The Yogafun method helps people learn how to relax, improve posture, strength, and flexibility, as well as calm their minds. Yogafun programs for kids, school teachers, and nurses are becoming popular as people look for various ways to relieve stress and tension.

Mindfulness Meditation

This type of meditation is based on mindfulness, which is a way of paying attention in an open and involved way. During mindfulness meditation, you can sit, walk, or engage in common activities such as eating, dressing, or cooking.

"In mindfulness practice, it is essential that you be fully engaged in the current moment, allowing thoughts and beliefs to come and go without judgment. This means being in touch with your feelings and accepting them with compassion for yourself. You can also choose to focus solely on your breath or on an idea or sensation. By bringing your attention back to this subject each time you feel restless or distracted, you learn to lengthen and integrate this skill into your daily life."

Practitioners say that the act of letting go or gently returning to the priority of the moment is essential when training. Formal meditation helps them to practice being present. It also helps you understand the importance of witnessing your thoughts and feelings and the role of the observer: you. Mindfulness meditation is considered a way to realise the essence of Buddhism, where attention and awareness activities handle the root causes of human suffering. Right and kind attention can enhance psychological health.

Transcendental Meditation

Transcendental Meditation is a unique practice originating from India and it relies on specific mantras or sounds. Often, each person goes through an interview with a group beforehand, and the invitation is issued to them based on that, as it needs to be a good fit. The technique first became known in the U.S. when The Beatles, the famous British pop band, travelled to Rishikesh in 1968 and spent several months learning the technique. They wrote many songs there which subsequently featured on their White Album, and it was partly due to their encouragement that the founder shifted his focus to the West.

The first course was taught in London in 1961 – even before The Beatles got involved with the practice. Now, there are millions of people who practice it. TM is said to allow your active mind to easily settle inward through quieter levels of thought until you experience the most silent and peaceful level of your own awareness — pure consciousness. This is different from mindfulness-based and Vipassana meditation, which involves a person's active focus on breathing. In fact, the "non-directive" techniques of TM are said to be fundamentally different from the "concentrative" practices of mindfulness and Vipassana. If the TM technique is truly unique, then the benefits it brings about should be different from other forms of meditation, and research has shown this to be the case. However, as with other meditation techniques, the only way for you to know if it will enhance your life is if you try it.

The TM technique requires learning from a qualified teacher. There are TM centres all around the world, and the course fee for learning is said to be towards the higher end of the scale. Once an individual has learned the technique, they can practice it on their own without the need for courses or further expenditure. The entire first course is taught over a 4-day period, and there are courses available each month. If you do not live close to a TM centre, you can also learn this meditation technique via an online course. Whilst it might be too complex and time-consuming to embark upon courses in TM, it is possible to use elements of it in daily life, using internet resources.

Most of the New Age meditations of various sorts, including those of Mindvalley and other contemporary mindfulness platforms such as Authentic Living and many others, use the TM meditation as a basis for their own guided meditations. Mindvalley (which you can easily find online) is an excellent platform offering a variety of grow quests, as they call them, for a relatively small fee. As I am a Mindvalley-certified Life Coach, of course, I am biased, so please make your own decisions. Mindvalley offers a system which it call a 6 Phase meditation, which can be easily found on YouTube. Have a look and listen and see if this would be something of help to you – it is for most people, and it is short.

Experiments with Light Meditations

I have also participated regularly in Quaker meditations, which have roots in Christian mysticism and go back to the founder of Quakers, George Fox, in the 17th century. Fundamentally, the practice encourages us to seek the Light through breathing and focused meditation in order to ask for divine guidance. Some might find this practice too much based on Christian tradition or too religious. However, again, I would recommend the experience, which can be very powerful. The Quaker Experiments with Light also have an element of sharing the experience and what one might call visions and words which come during it. The process of sharing the experience of the Light can feel like an uplifting and creative experience and all are welcome to it, regardless of their religion.

Loving-Kindness Meditation

Loving-kindness meditation is designed to uplift and open our hearts. It gently guides practitioners towards the development of compassion and love for themselves and others. During the practice, we recite phrases expressing goodwill. These phrases can be quite general, such as "May I be safe" or "May I be free from suffering." Feel free to generate your own phrases to suit your needs. By focusing on these phrases, we set an intention of kindness. Our attention is directed toward the feeling of the phrases instead of the verbal recitation of them. This meditation supports the healing of negative feelings and attitudes toward oneself. It also challenges individuals to extend themselves to others by silently reciting these phrases.

Reciting phrases of loving-kindness can help to transform negative thought patterns. In many studies, participants who have practised loving-kindness meditation improved their ability to read others' emotions compared to the other group. Through developing loving-kindness, positive relationships thrive. Not only does it increase happy feelings, but it helps to develop empathy. Some research suggests that it can help reduce anger and resentment. Although our feelings of anger and pain may become more challenging as we do this exercise, patience and self-forgiveness are key. Negative emotions are natural at first. This is often because the focus on love may bring up emotions and thoughts about love, including feelings of unworthiness, that we shy away from. With patience, they lose their force as we powerfully focus on bringing love in. In recent years, loving-kindness meditation has returned to Western society, where it's known as "metta" meditation. It is most commonly associated with Buddhist traditions of Southeast Asia where it is considered one of the oldest meditation practices. In its traditional form, loving-kindness is seen as a truly spiritual practice that has the potential to enhance a person's individual growth.

Start by choosing people in your life that have been a great source of love and support for you. This can be a parent, grandparent, friend, teacher, or anyone who fills your heart with joy. We use these people to generate a feeling of love in the heart. Then, we redirect that feeling to ourselves so that our self-image is touched by love. When loving-kindness meditation is practised consistently, it can contribute to the cultivation of a positive and nurturing connection with yourself, with others, and with the world around you.

How to Start a Meditation Practice

Starting to meditate can be a momentous occasion as well as a letdown. For many, the impetus to start comes from the many benefits of mindfulness and meditation. The downside comes when you want to start but can't seem to pinpoint exactly what to do. I have already mentioned various platforms, but there are literally hundreds now, and not all of them are respectable, so you need to choose them very carefully.

I do use some meditation in my life coaching practice alongside solid and more traditional coaching practices for the best results. The reason for it is a pragmatic goal-driven knowledge that meditation really can help shift your mood in no time at all.

If you are doing your meditations by yourself with no guiding presence, set realistic goals. If you think you will only benefit when you can sit perfectly still and reach a state of bliss, you are setting yourself up for disappointment. Like working out, the benefits of meditation are to be incorporated all along the journey. Meditation will increase focus and energy, decrease anxiety, enhance your well-being, and help you feel more grounded and connected the very first time you meditate. Most people, in fact, continue to meditate for these effects rather than for the allure of the mysterious, unbroken "bliss" state that flows from meditation. Don't set the bar too high for yourself! Do you have an insistent personality you must always appease and satisfy, or do you want some reliable resources for enjoying your days and making your life count most satisfyingly for you? Choose a consistent place and time. Finding a quiet and comfortable space that is free from external distractions can help to optimise and sustain your focus throughout your session. Experiment with different locations to determine where you feel most at ease and refreshed. Choose a time that suits you and your daily commitments. Whether it is in the mornings, evenings, or following a workout, morning routines play a crucial role in effectively setting your morning routine. While a set location in your home is ideal, you can substitute this with a quiet, comfortable chair or a favourite couch. It can also be helpful to maintain a straight posture to assist breathing techniques, especially if sitting for longer periods.

A meditation can be a powerful tool to regenerate your mind and empower you to take the next steps.

Tips for Overcoming Common Challenges in Meditation

Many people face common challenges when they first establish a meditation practice. They might experience restlessness or trouble sitting still, difficulties staying focused, having a mind that won't quiet down, doubts about their ability to meditate, or concerns about whether it is 'working' for them. Some people become concerned that meditative states might be a little like hysteria or hypnosis. It is understandable to worry about what might happen if we let go or if we give up control. Other people feel they are just bad at it or that time spent in meditation is not serving some more pressing need. There are as many variations as there are those who try it! The good news is that these experiences are normal. Almost everyone who meditates has some kind of difficulty or concern at some time or another. It is absolutely okay, and you are not alone.

There are many ways to work with these meditation challenges. As a general principle, try to be patient with yourself and not judge yourself too harshly. Remember that meditation is a practice, and we are learning how to do it. When we first learn something new, we are not usually very good at it. Meditation is no different. It is normal to experience difficulties and limitations. Limitations can be gateways to exploring new areas of development. So, a key principle is to take a growth mindset. This means remembering that difficulties are an unavoidable part of the learning process. There are several practical methods for working with our difficulties, including acknowledging a thought but not giving it relevance, letting go of distractions, or actively focusing on the motion of our breath. If you find yourself exhibiting many of these patterns, you might want to learn more in a course, a group such as a meditation or stress reduction group, or a club.

A final thought

As you navigate this transformative phase of your life, remember that seeking help is an integral part of the process. Embrace the resources available to you, whether through counselling, peer support, or wellness practices. By taking proactive steps to address your mental well-being and cultural adaptation, you lay the foundation for a fulfilling and successful academic journey. Trust in your ability to overcome obstacles, and allow yourself the grace to seek assistance when needed. In doing so, you not only pave your path to success but also inspire others to honour their own journeys.

Exercises: Cultivating Authenticity, Strength, Empathy, and Energetic Awareness

Cultivating Authenticity, Strength, and Empathy
Authenticity Exercise:

- Reflect on how your personal values have shaped your academic journey. Write about one key value (e.g., honesty, perseverance) that guided you through difficult times and how it influenced your decisions.

- Imagine yourself as a role model for others. What advice would you give to someone starting their PhD about staying authentic in their work and personal life?

Strength Exercise:

- Write about a time during your academic journey when you faced a major challenge but persevered. What did you learn about your inner strength, and how can you draw on that strength in future challenges?

- Create a 'strength inventory' by listing three personal qualities or skills that helped you succeed. For each one, write an example of when you used it effectively.

Empathy Exercise:

- Think about a moment when you showed empathy to a fellow student or colleague. What impact did your actions have on the other person, and what did you learn from the experience?

- Imagine you are mentoring a struggling international student. Write down three ways you could show empathy while helping them navigate their challenges.

Seeing from a Distance and Reframing Challenges

Seeing Others from a Distance:

- Imagine yourself observing a difficult interaction with someone (e.g., a critical supervisor or a challenging colleague) from a third-person perspective. Write about what you think might motivate their actions. Are they under pressure? Do they have personal or professional challenges you might not see?

- Reflect on how understanding their perspective changes your feelings about the situation. Write about one thing you could do to approach them with greater empathy.

Reframing Painful Experiences:

- Recall a particularly challenging situation you've faced during your academic journey. Instead of focusing on the discomfort, ask yourself: 'What lesson is the Universe trying to teach me through this experience?' Write about how this reframe changes your perspective.

- Identify a recent experience that upset you. What positive action or insight can you take away from it, knowing it was an opportunity for growth?

Exploring Energetic Empathy

Tuning into Energetic Empathy:

- Spend 5 minutes in a quiet space, focusing on someone you find challenging. Imagine their emotions as waves of energy moving outward. What do you sense about their energy? How might their experiences shape their actions?

- Reflect on your own energy. How does it shift when you think about the situation with empathy instead of frustration? Write down your insights.

Using Energetic Empathy for Growth:

- Visualise a difficult person surrounded by a soft, healing light. Imagine sending them positive energy and forgiveness. How does this exercise make you feel?

- Think of a time when someone extended understanding or forgiveness to you. How did it impact you? How can you use this memory to guide your approach to others?

Channeling Energy into Lessons:

- Identify a recurring challenge you've faced. Consider what energy you bring to the situation. What might you change to invite a better outcome?

- Write about one way you can use difficult interactions as lessons to deepen your understanding of yourself and others.

Chapter 6

INSPIRE AND BE INSPIRED: How to move from 'the survive' to 'the thrive' mode
Recognising Signs of Burnout

Recognising signs of burnout is a crucial skill that every international research scholar must develop to thrive in their academic journey. Burnout is not just fatigue; it manifests as emotional exhaustion, cynicism, and a diminished sense of personal accomplishment. As you navigate the complexities of research, cultural adjustments, and academic pressures, being attuned to these signs is essential. The earlier you recognise the symptoms, the more empowered you will be to address them effectively, ensuring that your passion for discovery remains alive and vibrant.

One of the most prominent signs of burnout is a pervasive sense of fatigue that doesn't seem to dissipate with rest. If you find yourself feeling drained after a full night's sleep or dreading the thought of getting back to your research, these could be red flags. This exhaustion can spread beyond the physical realm, affecting your mental sharpness and emotional resilience. Paying attention to these feelings is a vital step in acknowledging that something is amiss, and it's time to reevaluate your workload and self-care practices.

Another indicator of burnout is a growing sense of detachment from your work and colleagues. When you start to feel indifferent about your research or become disengaged from discussions that once excited you, it's essential to take a moment to reflect. This detachment can stem from feeling overwhelmed or unsupported in your academic environment. Connecting with peers and mentors can help alleviate these feelings, reminding you that you are not alone in this journey. Building a supportive network is crucial for fostering a sense of belonging and purpose in your work.

Irritability and mood swings are also common signs of burnout. If you notice that you are becoming short-tempered or unusually emotional, it might be time to take a step back. This emotional volatility can impact your relationships with fellow scholars and mentors, creating an isolating cycle that exacerbates the feelings of burnout. Practicing self-compassion and seeking out stress-reduction techniques, such as mindfulness or physical activity, can help you regain emotional balance and reconnect with your passion for research.

Lastly, a significant decrease in your productivity and creativity can signal that burnout is taking hold. When tasks that once inspired you now feel burdensome or when your innovative ideas seem to fade, it's essential to recognise this shift. Academic success is not solely measured by output but also by the joy and fulfilment derived from your work. Reassessing your goals, setting realistic expectations, and allowing yourself the grace to take breaks can reignite your motivation and inspire fresh perspectives. Embracing these strategies can transform your academic experience, turning challenges into opportunities for growth and renewal.

Work-Life Balance

Setting Boundaries Between Work and Personal Life

Setting boundaries between work and personal life is essential for international research scholars navigating the complexities of academia while adapting to a new culture. The pressure to excel academically can often blur the lines between professional obligations and personal time, leading to stress and burnout. By establishing clear boundaries, scholars can create a harmonious balance that fosters both academic success and personal well-being.

This balance is not merely a luxury but a necessity for sustaining long-term productivity and mental health.

To begin, it is crucial to define what boundaries mean in the context of your life as a research scholar. Boundaries are the limits you set around your time, energy, and emotional resources to protect your personal space. Start by identifying your priorities, both academically and personally. What tasks require your immediate attention? What activities rejuvenate your spirit? By understanding these priorities, you can allocate specific times for work and leisure, creating a structured schedule that respects both your professional goals and personal needs.

In the pursuit of academic excellence, it is easy to fall into the trap of overworking. The pressure to publish, attend conferences, and meet deadlines can make it seem impossible to take time for yourself. However, remember that rest and relaxation are integral to your productivity. Schedule regular breaks and stick to them, ensuring that you engage in activities that bring you joy outside of research. Whether it's exploring your new environment, connecting with friends, or practising a hobby, these moments of respite will recharge your mind and enhance your focus when you return to your work.

When you feel good and strong, try to inspire your peers. It is astonishing how much inspiring and helping other people can make you feel better. Try it! By now, you know so much more than most new students who arrive at a foreign university. Why not help them and inspire them to crate small support groups, discussion and mediation groups and self-help groups, as well as groups reaching out to life coaches. At The Scholars Mentor, we love groups of coaches, but the point is more general. Communication with peers, advisors, and family is another vital aspect of developing your well-being. Be open about your needs and limitations, but be bold and inspire others to find their voice and their values, and don't hesitate to express when you require time for personal commitments. This transparency not only fosters understanding but also cultivates a supportive environment where others can respect your boundaries. Remember that healthy relationships are built on mutual respect and understanding, and by sharing your journey, you may inspire others to prioritise their well-being as well.

Finally, in these aspirational inspirational gestures, be gentle with yourself as you navigate this balancing act. Adjusting to a new academic and cultural landscape can be daunting, but it is also exciting and if you do view the experiences as a joyful path, you will be rewarded in many ways. It is natural to experience challenges along the way. Embrace the learning process and recognise that setbacks are part of growth. By maintaining your boundaries and focusing on self-care, you will not only enhance your academic performance but also cultivate resilience and joy in your personal life. Ultimately, setting boundaries is not just about saying no; it is about saying yes to a fulfilling and balanced life that honours both your ambitions and your well-being.

The Role of Hobbies and Interests – how to help yourself feel inspired

Have fun! Hobbies and interests serve as a vital lifeline for international research scholars, offering a refreshing counterbalance to the rigours of academic life. Engaging in activities outside of one's primary research focus fosters creativity and innovation, essential traits for any successful scholar. When you immerse yourself in a hobby, whether it's painting, playing a musical instrument, or participating in sports, you tap into a different part of your brain that rejuvenates your spirit and enhances your productivity. These creative outlets can lead to breakthroughs in your research by allowing your mind to wander and explore new ideas in a relaxed state.

Cultivating hobbies is also a powerful tool for cultural adjustment and integration. As you navigate a new environment, engaging in local activities or joining clubs can help bridge cultural gaps and forge meaningful connections with peers. This engagement not only helps you understand your new surroundings better but also enriches your experience as an international scholar. Building friendships through shared interests can alleviate feelings of isolation, creating a supportive network that is crucial for maintaining mental well-being during challenging times.

Moreover, hobbies and interests provide a necessary respite from the pressures of academic work, acting as a form of stress relief. The demands of research can often feel overwhelming, leading to burnout if not managed effectively. By dedicating time to pursue something you love, you create a buffer against stress, allowing your mind to recharge. This practice of self-care is fundamental to sustaining your passion for research and ensuring long-term academic success. As you engage in these activities, you not only improve your mental health but also develop essential life skills, such as time management and discipline.

In conclusion, embracing hobbies and interests is not merely a leisure activity; it is a strategic approach to navigating the complexities of academic life as an international research scholar. By recognising the multifaceted benefits that these pursuits offer, you empower yourself to create a fulfilling and enriching experience. As you continue on your academic journey, let your passions guide you, bolstering your resilience and creativity and ultimately leading you to greater success in both your research and personal life.

This is myself with my former PhD student Dr Charmaine Dambuza Kundai. We are now firm friends and collaborators.

Time for Family and Friends

In the whirlwind of academic pursuits, it is easy for international research scholars to become engulfed in their studies, often at the expense of personal relationships. However, the time spent with family and friends is not merely a distraction; it is an essential pillar of well-being and success. By nurturing these connections, scholars can cultivate a support system that provides emotional resilience, a sense of belonging, and a much-needed reprieve from the pressures of academic life. Embracing this balance can ultimately lead to greater productivity and creativity in research.

Family and friends enrich our lives in ways that go beyond mere companionship. They offer perspectives that challenge our thinking and inspire us to grow. Engaging with loved ones allows scholars to share their experiences, reflect on their journeys and celebrate milestones together. These interactions serve as reminders of the greater purpose behind academic endeavours. While the pursuit of knowledge is significant, it is the relationships we build along the way that truly define our experiences and successes.

Moreover, time spent with loved ones is a powerful antidote to stress. Engaging in social activities, whether it be a simple meal, a hike, or a game night, allows the mind to recharge and rejuvenate. These moments of joy and laughter serve as reminders that life exists beyond the confines of academia. A balanced life, enriched with meaningful relationships, equips scholars to approach their research with renewed vigour and focus. The emotional support from family and friends not only alleviates stress but also enhances mental well-being, fostering a healthier work-life balance essential for academic success.

Ultimately, the journey of an international research scholar is not just about achieving academic milestones but also about creating memories and connections that last a lifetime. By prioritising time for family and friends, scholars can cultivate a fulfilling life that harmonises personal and academic aspirations. Embracing this balance will not only enrich your experience but also enhance your ability to contribute positively to your field and community. Remember, success is not solely measured by accolades but by the relationships that sustain and uplift you along the way.

EXERCISES:

Celebrating Small Wins

Every step forward counts. Today, we focus on celebrating even the smallest achievements, as they all contribute to your larger goal.

Exercise

1. Think about a small win you've experienced in the past week—whether academic or personal. Write it down.

2. Reflect on how this small win contributes to your overall success. Write about how it made you feel.

3. Celebrate this small win today by taking a moment to acknowledge your achievement. Treat yourself to something enjoyable, or share the win with someone who supports you.

4. Write about how celebrating small wins helps you stay motivated.

Reflection

What did celebrating a small win teach you about the importance of recognising progress?

Finding Strength in Vulnerability

True strength often lies in our vulnerability. Today, we explore how embracing vulnerability can help you grow stronger and more resilient.

Exercise

1. Reflect on a time when you felt vulnerable in your academic or personal life. Write about how this experience made you feel.

2. Think about how you handled that vulnerability. Did it lead to personal growth, connection with others, or new insights?

3. Now, reflect on a current situation where you feel vulnerable. How can you embrace this vulnerability as a source of strength?

4. Write down one action you can take today that embraces vulnerability with grace.

Reflection

How does embracing vulnerability empower you? How can you use vulnerability to build resilience in your journey?

Creating Lasting Habits

Habits shape our daily lives and contribute to long-term success. Today, we focus on identifying and creating habits that will support your personal and academic goals.

Exercise

1. Think about one habit you'd like to establish (e.g., journaling, exercise, or reading). Write down why it's important to you.
2. Break this habit down into smaller steps. What can you do each day to build it into your routine?
3. Set a specific, achievable goal for the next week related to this habit. Write down one action you can take today to begin.
4. Reflect on how this new habit will support your personal growth and academic success.

Reflection

How will establishing this habit impact your life? What benefits do you anticipate it bringing to your journey?

Chapter 7

ORGANISE; Developing a Growth Mindset
Developing a Growth Mindset

In terms of my LION methodology we have focused quite a lot on the LEARNING and the INSPIRING. Now the time has come for organising your mind so you can become the master of your thoughts rather than pawn on the chessboard of uncontrollable emotions.

Growth Mindset is the belief that abilities and intelligence can be developed through dedication, effort, and learning from experience. Unlike a fixed mindset, which assumes that talent and capacity are static, a growth mindset embraces challenges, sees failure as an opportunity for growth, and fosters resilience in the face of setbacks.

Philosophically, a growth mindset aligns with the idea that human potential is not predetermined—it is dynamic and constantly evolving. This mindset encourages an openness to new experiences and a willingness to step outside one's comfort zone, recognising that **progress is a process, not a destination.**

For international researchers, cultivating a growth mindset is crucial. It transforms challenges into opportunities for development, fosters adaptability, and supports long-term success in unfamiliar academic environments.

Embracing a growth mindset means recognising and understanding that abilities and intelligence can be developed and enhanced through dedication, effort, and deep reflection. This perspective not only fosters resilience and perseverance but also encourages a deep love for learning and a passionate commitment to progress. As you embark on your research journey and dive into your studies, understanding that challenges are actually opportunities for growth and development will empower you to effectively overcome obstacles and achieve both your academic and personal goals in a meaningful way.

In the realm of research, setbacks are inevitable. Whether it's a failed experiment, an unresponsive advisor, or cultural misunderstandings, these experiences can be discouraging. However, viewing these challenges through the lens of a growth mindset transforms them into valuable learning experiences. Each setback is a stepping stone that can provide insights into your research process, improve your problem-solving skills, and enhance your adaptability. By reframing failures as opportunities for learning, you cultivate resilience, which is crucial for thriving in a demanding academic environment.

Cultivating a growth mindset also involves surrounding yourself with a supportive community. Engage with fellow international scholars who share similar experiences and challenges. This network can provide encouragement, share strategies for overcoming cultural barriers, and foster a sense of belonging. Collaboration and open discussions can lead to innovative ideas and solutions that enhance your research work. Remember, you are not alone in this journey; leveraging the strength of your peers can bolster your confidence and reinforce the belief that growth is possible. It is here too that some find a belief in higher benevolent power helpful, but you can choose to believe in your own power of transformation, supported by loved ones and your mentors. I do not use the word 'God' in my coaching practice – I do believe that the Universe is benevolent and that quantum physics teaches us that there is a lot we do not know. Mostly, I believe in love and the power of creation based on your core values.

Prioritise self-compassion in your growth journey. As you pursue academic excellence, it's easy to be overly critical of yourself. Instead, treat yourself with the same kindness you would offer a friend facing challenges. Recognise that every scholar experiences struggles and these moments do not define your worth or potential. By fostering a nurturing internal dialogue, you encourage perseverance and resilience, enabling you to embrace challenges with enthusiasm and a deep-seated belief in your capacity for growth and success.

Celebrating Small Wins - again

Celebrating small wins is a crucial practice in the journey of international research scholars, who often face unique challenges while navigating their academic and cultural environments. Each small achievement, whether it's completing a challenging piece of research, mastering a new language skill, or simply acclimating to a different culture, deserves recognition. These milestones, though they may seem minor in the grand scheme of academic pursuits, are the building blocks of resilience and motivation. Acknowledging these victories not only reinforces your commitment to your goals but also nurtures a sense of belonging and purpose in your academic journey.

In the demanding world of academia, where the pressure to produce significant results can feel overwhelming, it is essential to shift the focus from solely pursuing major achievements to appreciating the incremental progress made along the way. Each step forward, no matter how small, contributes to your overall growth and success. By celebrating these small wins, you create a positive feedback loop that boosts your confidence and enhances your overall well-being. This practice helps cultivate a mindset that values persistence and perseverance, essential traits for any researcher navigating the complexities of their field.

Moreover, celebrating small victories fosters a sense of community and connection among international scholars. Sharing your achievements with peers can strengthen relationships and create a supportive environment where everyone feels valued. Whether it's through informal gatherings, social media, or academic networks, expressing joy in one another's accomplishments helps build a culture of encouragement and collaboration. This sense of camaraderie can be particularly beneficial for those adjusting to new cultural contexts, as it promotes integration and a feeling of belonging within the academic community.

Incorporating the celebration of small wins into your routine can be both simple and impactful. Consider setting aside time each week to reflect on your progress, whether it involves journaling, discussing achievements with a mentor, or engaging in self-affirmation practices. These moments of reflection not only reinforce your successes but also provide an opportunity to assess your goals and realign your focus as needed. Engaging in these practices can transform your approach to research, shifting the narrative from one of struggle to one filled with hope and accomplishment.

At times, anybody can feel angry at the various setbacks and injustices that have come our way. Many of us have been taught that anger is bad and destructive, and it can be. My view is that it is important to recognise and acknowledge anger and perhaps work through it in a creative and constructive way. We have already mentioned empathy, which can be used to diffuse negative feelings without denying the pain and frustration. Anger can also be our fuel to keep going. You do not need to act on it – or to be violent in whichever way, either verbally or actually – but at times recognising one's anger to sublimate this into a powerful sense of empathy and transformation. In some cultures, women are simply not allowed to be angry, and in those cultures in particular, it is most important that anger is recognised and owned and even treated as a special power that one can step into.

Ultimately, the journey of an international research scholar is a tapestry woven with both challenges and triumphs. By consciously celebrating small wins, you cultivate a resilient mindset that embraces the journey rather than solely fixating on the destination. Each small victory is a testament to your dedication, adaptability, and growth. As you navigate the intricacies of academic life, remember that every step you take is significant, and each celebration serves as a reminder that you are not just surviving but thriving in your pursuit of knowledge and success.

Exercises:

Using Anger for Good

Anger and frustration are natural parts of who we are. Today, we focus on how to use these emotions constructively by incorporating them into our journey and transforming them into empathy and positive energy.

Exercise

1. Close your eyes and think about a time when you felt angry or frustrated recently.

2. Reflect on the underlying reasons for your anger. Is it due to unmet expectations, external pressure, or internal conflict?

3. Now, imagine that anger transforming into light. Visualise it as a powerful, golden energy that fills your body and radiates outward.

4. With each exhale, imagine releasing any negativity associated with the anger, letting it dissolve into the light.

5. End by reflecting on how you can channel this energy into positive actions today. Perhaps it's in your work, relationships, or personal growth.

Reflection

How did it feel to transform your anger into light? What action will you take today to use that energy constructively?

Rest and Recharge

It's natural to feel tired at times. Today, we focus on the importance of rest while also staying physically active and reflecting on the many blessings in your life.

Exercise

1. Take a moment to recognise any tiredness or fatigue you may be feeling. Allow yourself to acknowledge it without judgment.

2. Set aside time today to rest—whether it's a nap, a break, or simply stepping away from work.

3. As you rest, think about your physical activity. Even a short walk can help rejuvenate you and clear your mind. Go outside if possible.

4. While walking, reflect on at least three blessings in your life. Write them down and notice how your perspective shifts.

5. Write about how you can balance rest and activity in the future. What will you do to ensure your energy is nurtured?

Reflection

How does recognising both the need for rest and physical activity balance your energy? How can you maintain this going forward?

Finding Motivation in Your Progress

When the path gets tough, it's essential to recognise your progress. Today, we celebrate the steps you've already taken and use them as motivation to keep moving forward.

Exercise

1. Take a moment to reflect on your journey so far. Write down three significant achievements or breakthroughs you've made in your PhD journey.

2. For each one, write a brief reflection on the effort, perseverance, or insight it took to achieve it.

3. Think about a time you felt particularly motivated. What triggered that motivation? Write about it.

4. Use this reflection to create an affirmation or mantra that reminds you of how far you've come.

Reflection

How does recognising your progress affect your motivation? How can you keep this sense of accomplishment alive?

Connecting Body, Spirit, and Intellect

Your body, spirit, and intellect are all interconnected. Today, we explore how integrating these aspects of yourself can help you stay balanced and focused on your goals.

Exercise

1. Sit in a comfortable position, close your eyes, and take a few deep breaths.
2. Focus on the sensations in your body. Notice how it feels in the present moment—your posture, the energy you're holding, and any tension.
3. Now, bring your thoughts to your spirit. How does it feel to connect with your higher purpose or your inner self? Write about what comes up.
4. Reflect on how your intellect, body, and spirit all contribute to your ability to pursue your PhD. How can you nurture each of these to stay balanced?
5. Visualise these three parts of yourself working in harmony as you pursue your goals.

Reflection

How did this exercise change your perception of yourself? How can you ensure that body, spirit, and intellect stay in alignment throughout your journey?

Chapter 8

ORGANISE MORE: Networking and Collaboration
The Power of Professional Relationships

We have looked at various aspects of this journey, and the notion of organisation, of course, extends beyond your mind – it has to extend to the so-called 'real life.' Your journey as an international research student is about so much more than just academic rigour—it's a path filled with challenges, discoveries, and opportunities for growth. And here's the main secret which you do know already: you don't have to do it alone.

The professional relationships you build along the way will be your greatest asset. A strong network of supportive colleagues, mentors, and advisors will not only enrich your academic experience but also safeguard your well-being. These connections will serve as your safety net, offering guidance, encouragement, and that essential sense of belonging in a world that may, at times, feel unfamiliar.

So, seek out mentors who truly understand what it means to walk this path as an international scholar. The right mentor can be a game-changer—someone who helps you navigate institutional expectations, offers thoughtful feedback on your research and introduces you to invaluable professional networks. Their wisdom can reveal doors you never even knew existed, and their support will help you stay steady when doubt creeps in. Be bold in reaching out, and don't settle for mentorship that doesn't align with your goals and values. Find those who inspire you and let their experience fuel your own growth.

And don't forget your peers. The friendships and collaborations you forge with fellow international students will be a lifeline. Together, you can navigate the ups and downs of research life, exchange ideas, and create something greater than what any one of you could achieve alone. Lean into these relationships. Celebrate the richness of different perspectives, challenge each other, and push the boundaries of what's possible. Innovation thrives on diversity, and your peers bring with them a world of knowledge that can reshape how you approach your work.

So, step forward. Build your network, embrace mentorship, and cherish collaboration. These relationships will not only carry you through your research but also shape the scholar—and the person—you are becoming.

Finding Mentors and Sponsors

Finding mentors and sponsors is a pivotal step in the journey of international research scholars. As you navigate the complexities of academia and cultural landscapes, having the right guidance can illuminate your path and enhance your growth. Mentors are invaluable sources of wisdom, offering insights drawn from their own experiences, while sponsors actively advocate for your advancement. Together, they create a powerful support system that fosters your academic and personal development, helping you to overcome challenges and seize opportunities.

To identify potential mentors and sponsors, begin by assessing your network. Look around you—professors, senior researchers, and even peers can serve as mentors. Engage with faculty members whose work resonates with your interests. Attend seminars, workshops, and conferences to broaden your connections. The more you immerse yourself in your academic community, the more likely you'll encounter individuals who can offer support. Don't hesitate to reach out; a simple email expressing admiration for their work or seeking advice can open doors to meaningful relationships.

Once you've identified potential mentors, approach them with authenticity and respect. Prepare for meetings by having clear questions or topics for discussion, demonstrating your seriousness and commitment to your research. Be open and willing to share your experiences as an international scholar. This transparency will help foster a genuine connection and allow your mentor to understand your unique challenges and aspirations. Remember, mentorship is a two-way street; while you are seeking guidance, be prepared to contribute to the relationship by sharing insights and feedback.

Besides mentorship, seek out sponsors who can advocate for your work and help elevate your profile within your field. Sponsors often have influence and connections that can lead to opportunities such as research grants, positions on committees, or invitations to speak at conferences. Building these relationships requires ongoing engagement and the demonstration of your capabilities. Show your dedication through your work, be it through collaborative projects or by volunteering for departmental activities, showcasing your skills and commitment to your academic community.

Last, as you cultivate these essential relationships, remember to maintain a balance between professional development and personal well-being. The process of finding mentors and sponsors should not add to your stress but rather enhance your academic journey. Take time for self-care and reflection, ensuring that your pursuit of guidance aligns with your values and goals. Embrace the support network you create, and allow it to inspire and propel you forward in your academic endeavours, ultimately leading to a successful and fulfilling experience as an international research scholar.

Engaging in Collaborative Research

Engaging in collaborative research can be a transformative experience for international research scholars, providing not only a pathway to academic excellence but also a rich tapestry of cultural exchange and personal growth. When you join forces with peers from diverse backgrounds, you open the door to innovative ideas and methodologies that can enhance your own research. This collaborative spirit fosters an environment where knowledge is shared freely, leading to breakthroughs that might not be possible in isolation. Embrace the potential of these partnerships to enrich your academic journey and cultivate a sense of belonging within the global academic community.

As you navigate the complexities of collaborative research, it is important to recognise the unique strengths each team member brings to the table. Celebrate the diverse perspectives that arise from different cultural contexts, as these differences can spark creativity and expand the horizons of your research. Foster an atmosphere of mutual respect and open dialogue where every voice is valued. This inclusivity not only enhances the quality of your work but also builds lasting relationships that can support both your academic and personal development. In this way, collaboration becomes a powerful tool for integration into your new environment.

Faced with challenges, such as language barriers or differing academic practices, view these obstacles as opportunities for growth. Effective communication is essential in collaborative settings, and honing your skills in this area can lead to improved relationships and increased confidence in your academic abilities. Seek out resources, such as workshops or mentorship programs, that can help you develop your communication strategies. Remember, every effective collaboration begins with a willingness to listen and learn from one another. This mindset fosters resilience and adaptability, qualities that are invaluable in both research and life.

Taking on collaborative projects can also help you manage the stresses associated with research. When you work with others, you distribute the workload and share the emotional burden of challenges that arise during the research process. This camaraderie can lead to a more balanced research experience, allowing you to maintain your mental well-being and work-life balance. Engage regularly with your collaborators, not just in academic discussions but also in social settings. Building friendships within your research team can create a supportive network that buffers against stress and enhances overall satisfaction in your academic journey.

Ultimately, engaging in collaborative research is about more than just producing results; it's about the connections you make and the personal growth you experience along the way. Each collaboration offers a chance to learn more about yourself and others, to challenge your assumptions, and to expand your worldview. As you immerse yourself in these experiences, keep in mind that success is not solely measured by academic achievements but also by the relationships you nurture and the impact you have on those around you.

Embrace the journey of collaboration, and let it guide you toward a fulfilling and successful academic career.

Exercises:

Embracing the Present Moment

The present moment is where life happens. Today, we practice embracing the now as a way to reduce anxiety about the future.

Exercise

1. Sit quietly and close your eyes. Take slow, deep breaths, focusing on the sensation of your breath entering and leaving your body.

2. Notice the sounds, sensations, and smells around you. Allow yourself to be fully present without judgment.

3. Reflect on something positive about this moment—what can you appreciate right now?

4. Write about this experience and how it felt to embrace the present moment fully.

Reflection

How did focusing on the present moment affect your state of mind? How can you bring this practice into your daily life?

Defining Your Success

Success means different things to different people. Today, we define what success looks like for you based on your values and goals.

Exercise

1. Take a moment to write down your definition of success. What does it look like in your academic, personal, and professional life?

2. Reflect on how this definition aligns with your values. Are there areas where it feels out of sync?

3. Write down three specific goals that reflect your personal definition of success.

4. Reflect on one action you can take this week to move closer to these goals.

Reflection

What did defining success teach you about your values and priorities? How does this clarity help you focus?

Chapter 9

NAVIGATING THROUGH SURRENDER:
Radical Gratitude: growth through challenging times

Introduction: The Power of Perspective

'Radical gratitude' is a relatively new concept drawing from various philosophies, including Buddhism, Christianity, and New Age approaches, which, in essence, encourages an individual to be grateful for anything in life and to use the experience as a journey and a tool for growth. Some people find the notion of 'radical gratitude' improbable, whilst others advocate its power for good. Try it! Be grateful for whatever comes your way and treat it as a lesson and a chance to practice your curiosity that will lead to spiritual and material abundance. Most people can feel some kind of gratitude when things go well, although it never ceases to amaze how many people just take their good fortune for granted until it all goes horribly wrong). The idea of radical gratitude is precisely that - it is radical and hard as you are expected to feel gratitude even as things go awry. How and why? Let me explain.

As an international research student, your academic journey is both an adventure and a challenge. It is an exciting opportunity to expand your knowledge, push boundaries, and contribute to the world. Yet, it is also filled with moments of uncertainty, doubt, and, at times, loneliness. These challenges can weigh heavily on your mind and spirit. But amid these difficulties, there lies an incredibly powerful tool—Radical Gratitude.

What Is Radical Gratitude?

Radical Gratitude goes beyond the traditional understanding of being thankful for the positive things in life. It is not simply about recognising good things in life but rather learning how to see the value in every experience, perhaps especially the difficult ones. Radical Gratitude asks us to embrace all of life—both the highs and the lows—and to find wisdom in every moment. It invites us to reflect on how each experience, each setback, and each challenge contributes to our personal and academic growth. I need to confess that I have tried hard to practice 'radical gratitude' but still, at times, get angry and frustrated. However, my experience of even trying it has been empowering as it makes you feel you are taking charge or at least attempting to. The cornerstone of Radical Gratitude is a belief that there is a higher power at work and that the Universe is benign.

For international research students, many of whom face cultural adjustment, language barriers, and academic pressure, Radical Gratitude can become a transformative tool. It encourages you to look at every challenge as an opportunity for learning rather than as a threat. Radical Gratitude teaches us to approach hard moments, and even moments of failure, with curiosity and openness, recognising that they are part of the journey and can lead to unexpected breakthroughs. It is an exciting proposition, but it is not easy.

Learning from Setbacks: Every Obstacle Might Be a Lesson

In academic life, setbacks are inevitable. Whether it's the pressure of writing a dissertation, navigating unfamiliar academic systems, or struggling to communicate in a second language, challenges will arise. Radical gratitude asks us to treat these challenges not as setbacks or roadblocks—they are the very things that push you to grow. Even the knowledge that such an attitude exists might be a helpful tool.

When you practice Radical Gratitude, you are invited to change the way you view these obstacles. Instead of seeing them as insurmountable problems, you start to see them as lessons that can teach you valuable skills:

resilience, patience, empathy, and problem-solving. A failed experiment, an unexpected critique from a supervisor, or a miscommunication can all serve as opportunities to refine your skills, sharpen your thinking, and strengthen your character.

For example, when faced with a language barrier, instead of feeling defeated, Radical Gratitude invites you to appreciate the opportunity to develop further communication skills. It encourages you to reflect on how mastering this challenge will make you a better scholar and a more effective teacher, able to bridge cultural gaps with ease. Yes, I hear you say, but what about the real challenges of life? What about your lover leaving you for another, for example? How can you possibly see it as a useful lesson? Radical Gratitude asks exactly that – treat the worst experience as a lesson and an opportunity to grow. I can feel you saying to me, 'A language barrier is a little different from a broken heart.' Yes it is, but Radical Gratitude invites you also to believe in hope and Light: things will work out if you let them and if you take steps to develop and grow. Maybe your unfaithful lover was not the right person for you after all. Maybe this opportunity gives you a chance to look at yourself in terms of your choices and inner expectations of love, and just perhaps it offers you a place to grow and, in time, find a more suitable person.

The Role of Anxiety: Embracing It, Not Avoiding It

Anxiety happens to most people. Anxiety is also a natural part of the academic journey. – it can feel like a rising and paralysing fear which engulfs our every cell. 'A panic attack' can feel like a heart attack – that is something that is a suffocating, aggressive invasion of who we are. It is not a good thing. The pressure to succeed, the fear of failure, and the overwhelming workload can all lead to feelings of nervousness and stress. For international students, there may also be the added weight of adjusting to a new cultural and academic environment. While anxiety can feel uncomfortable, it is important to acknowledge it and not let it freeze your mind or paralyze your intellectual abilities. Anxiety, when not acknowledged and *'tamed,'* could become your real enemy, something that stops you from doing anything at all.

Radical Gratitude teaches us that it is okay to experience anxiety, as it is a universal human emotion. It is like in that famous Simon and Garfunkel song 'Hello Darkness My Old Friend.' If we treat darkness and anxiety as a friend, if we recognise it, we can do something with it. Rather than trying to eliminate it entirely, Radical Gratitude encourages us to use anxiety as a tool for awareness. Darkness, after all, is simply a light forgotten or hidden temporarily. Anxiety often signals that we care deeply about our work or that we are stepping into unfamiliar territory. It is a sign that a change, a transformation, in short personal growth is taking place.

Instead of allowing anxiety to control you, Radical Gratitude gives you the ability to use it as fuel. By practising mindfulness, grounding techniques, and positive self-talk, you can calm your nerves, focus your mind, and use that energy to push through challenges rather than letting them overwhelm you.

Building a Resilient Mindset: The Foundation of Success

The key takeaway from Radical Gratitude is that it strengthens your mindset – if you let it. In academic and personal life, a strong mindset is your greatest ally. It is the foundation that allows you to persevere when the going gets tough, bounce back after setbacks, and stay focused on your long-term goals. When you approach challenges with Radical Gratitude, you develop a mindset that is flexible, open, and solution-oriented.

One of the most important aspects of Radical Gratitude is the ability to be present. What does this mean? It means to be in the moment, not on your phone, not scrolling, not staring at screens hoping to numb your pain – Radical Gratitude invites you to be in the moment right now. As you continue your academic journey, it's easy to become consumed by the future—completing your dissertation, landing a job, or securing funding. While these goals are important, Radical Gratitude encourages you to stay grounded in the present moment and continue to ask yourself, 'Who am I?' 'Why am I here?' 'where am I going?' It reminds you that growth occurs in the here and now, not just in the future. It is another step into this elusive life purpose concept which makes it all worthwhile.

By focusing on your feelings just now and on what you are learning or might be learning, rather than what you lack or where you feel behind, you create a resilient mindset that helps you to stay steady and also work towards your abundance. "Abundance' can mean – and, in my view – must mean – a number of different things. To some people, it just means money and material abundance, but it really ought to be treated as a pathway to a rich life, surrounded by family and friends with adventures and opportunities to be generous and kind.

Every day becomes an opportunity to move closer to your goals, not because you are perfect or without struggle, but because you are willing to embrace each step of the process with gratitude.

Radical Gratitude as a Tool for Mental Well-Being

As I have mentioned at the very outset of this volume, for international students, mental well-being is a critical concern. The pressures of academia, the sense of isolation, and the feeling of being "other" can take a toll on your mental health. I have already suggested a variety of other tools, including meditation, networking, peer support, seeking help in the form of counselling and life coaching etc. This is another step: if you can master this (perhaps using all the other steps mentioned in this book), Radical Gratitude provides a tool for healthily managing these pressures.

By cultivating a mindset of gratitude, you begin to focus on what is working in your life—your achievements, your strengths, and the support systems you've built. Are things which are not working some inexplicable punishments? Or do you have anything to do with these occurring, too? This you can ask yourself lovingly – no judgement, but let's learn. This shift in focus helps to combat feelings of anxiety, depression, or imposter syndrome. It allows you to see that, despite challenges, you are making progress and you are capable of achieving your goals.

Radical Gratitude does not dismiss the reality of mental health challenges, and clearly, if your darkness becomes impossible to tame, you must consult your doctor and find clinical solutions. However, I do believe that there is a liminal space between that dire situation and feeling upset and anxious – and I do believe you can dispel the dark clouds through meditation, talking to a life coach, talking to your friends and feeling grateful for being on this planet at all and for being given an opportunity to create the life that you desire. Radical Gratitude offers a proactive approach to maintaining balance. It empowers you to take action—whether it's seeking support, practising self-compassion, or engaging in activities that promote well-being—while also acknowledging that these struggles are part of the human experience.

Conclusion: Thriving Through Setbacks

As you move forward in your academic journey, remember that Radical Gratitude is not just a tool for surviving difficult times but for thriving in them. This attitude might allow you to embrace challenges more vigorously, learn from setbacks, and cultivate resilience. It helps you to view every experience as a chance for growth, whether it is a success or a struggle.

Through Radical Gratitude, you are empowered to build a strong, balanced mindset that supports both your intellectual and personal growth. You can acknowledge anxiety as part of the process and still move forward with clarity and focus. By embracing this practice, you create a foundation for success—not only in your academic endeavours but in life itself.

You are on a journey that will not only lead to academic achievement but also personal transformation. Each step, no matter how difficult, is a part of your path to becoming the scholar and individual you are meant to be.

In this volume, I shared with you a variety of reflections on the journey of an international research student and several tools which will make this journey easier. Clearly, it is up to each and every individual to find their own pathway to success and to find their own peace and harmony in life, whether they are a research student or simply a human being looking for answers to live a better and more peaceful life.

It is my belief that all these tools, together when applied, will amount to a sense of Radical Gratitude and through Radical Gratitude, you will find the strength to navigate the academic (and the life) journey with confidence, resilience, and joy.

If you want a further discussion with no obligation or fee, do drop me and my team a line through LinkedIn or www.scholarsmentor.com.

Final Exercises for Radical Gratitude

Exercise 1: Radical Gratitude for Challenges

Introduction:

Sit down in a quiet room and identify the core challenge you are facing. Is it a difficult supervisor (or another person?) Is it a sense that you are homesick and there is nothing you can do about it? Do you miss your first language (your mother tongue?)

Steps:

1. Write the core challenge down on a piece of paper. Try to think about the challenge from a different perspective. To do this, imagine yourself moving further away from your piece of paper and

seeing this from a bigger perspective physically. Perhaps the language difficulties might open a door for acquiring linguistic skills further. Perhaps your difficult supervisor can be seen as somebody who is not big and scary but rather an individual with issues of their own – you can learn to learn from them only the skill that benefits you and leave the fear and annoyance aside.

2. Write about the emotions you are experiencing at the beginning of the exercise and as you move away from it in your mind.

3. Now, shift your perspective again and come close again: What is this challenge teaching you? Write three lessons you can learn from this experience.

4. Finally, express gratitude for the opportunity to learn these lessons. Even in difficult times, there is always something valuable to take away.

Reflection:

How did reframing this challenge help you feel? What new insights did you gain from this exercise?

Exercise 2: Acknowledging and Embracing Anxiety

Introduction:

I hate feeling anxious and so do you, I am sure. The sense of some kind of doom approaches at times with no good reason and no resolution. Anxiety is a natural part of the human experience, especially in high-pressure academic environments. This exercise teaches you to dispel the sense of doom and attempts to transform and acknowledge anxiety as a part of the journey and use it as a source of motivation rather than stress.

Steps:

1. Close your eyes and take a few deep breaths. Acknowledge any anxiety you are feeling.

2. Without judgment, write down the sources of your anxiety. What are you afraid of? If you cannot identify exactly why you are anxious, do write down 'I do not know.'

3. Reframe your anxiety as a signal that you care deeply about your work. Write about how this anxiety is, in fact, a sign you care deeply about your research and about how it will affect you and your

family. Feel proud that you are so caring. Smile and tell yourself this anxiety can be used as fuel for growth.

4. Open your eyes and stretch and tell yourself that you are not anxious anymore. Take small steps today to move through this anxiety. Put a high energy music on and dance to it. Write how this has made you feel and take steps to move forward with clarity.

Reflection:

How does acknowledging and reframing your anxiety make you feel? How can you use anxiety as a tool for growth moving forward?

Exercise 3: Gratitude Journaling for Growth

Introduction:

Throughout this book, I have suggested that identifying the ways you feel is an important step in choosing the emotions you feel. Journaling can be a powerful tool for cultivating Radical Gratitude. This exercise helps you reflect on the day and find things to be grateful for, even in the face of challenges. The most important thing to be grateful for is the sheer fact that you are alive and have a chance to experience so many things.

Steps:

1. Set aside 10 minutes each day to journal. Write about three things you are grateful for today—big or small.
2. Reflect on how each of these things has contributed to your growth or well-being.
3. Write about one challenge you faced today and how it helped you grow. Express gratitude for the lesson it provided.
4. End with an affirmation of gratitude for your progress and the opportunity to continue learning.

Reflection:

How does gratitude journaling shift your mindset? What new insights did you gain from this exercise?

Practising radical gratitude is not easy but can alter our mindset and deliver powerful connections to the spiritual realm

Chapter 10

NAVIGATE YOUR NEXT STEPS: Looking Ahead

Preparing for Life After Academia

You have done so much already, and your journey has been amazing. You are now approaching the end of the challenging path and you can see the finishing line right ahead of you! Well done. And now what? Navigating your next steps is a crucial moment and many (far too many people) drop out at the last hurdle or get discouraged before the finishing line, or somehow collapse after the finish. What now?

Preparing for life after academia is a crucial step in the journey of every international research scholar. Transitioning from the structured environment of academia to the vast and often unpredictable world beyond can be daunting. However, this phase also presents a unique opportunity to reflect on your experiences, harness your skills, and chart a course toward fulfilling and meaningful endeavours. Embrace this time as a moment to envision your future, recognising that your academic journey has equipped you with valuable insights and competencies that can be applied in diverse contexts.

As you prepare for this transition, it is essential to engage in self-reflection. Consider your academic achievements, the research projects you've completed, and the skills you've developed along the way. These elements form the foundation of your professional identity. Take time to identify what aspects of your research ignited your passion and what skills you enjoyed utilising most. This process will not only help you understand your strengths but will also guide you in making informed decisions about your next steps, whether that means pursuing a career in academia, industry, or other fields.

Networking is another vital component of preparing for life after academia. Building relationships with professionals in your field can provide invaluable insights and open doors to opportunities that may not be immediately visible. Attend conferences, workshops, and seminars to connect with industry leaders and fellow scholars. Utilise platforms like LinkedIn to engage with alumni from your institution and explore potential career paths. Remember, each connection you make is a step toward expanding your horizons and understanding the landscape of the professional world you are about to enter.

Cultural adjustment plays a significant role in this transition as well. As an international research scholar, you may have faced challenges in adapting to a new environment, and these cultural nuances will continue to influence your career journey. Embracing the diversity of experiences you've encountered will not only enrich your perspective but also enhance your adaptability in various professional settings. Seek out mentorship and support from those who understand the complexities of navigating different cultural contexts, as their guidance can be instrumental in building confidence and resilience as you forge your path forward.

Finally, prioritise your mental well-being and work-life balance as you approach this new chapter. The pressures of academic life can often lead to stress and burnout, making it essential to develop strategies for maintaining a healthy equilibrium. Engage in practices that promote mindfulness and self-care, such as exercise, meditation, and social activities that bring you joy. Establishing boundaries between work and personal life will help you transition more smoothly into your next phase. By taking care of yourself and nurturing your passions outside of academia, you will be better equipped to embrace the opportunities and challenges that lie ahead, ultimately leading to a fulfilling and successful life beyond the academic realm.

Setting Long-Term Goals

We have already discussed the notion of visualising your future and your Life Purpose, which must align with your values and contribute to society as a whole – I am saying this not to be judgmental but simply to empower you to take these extra steps.

Setting long-term goals is a powerful catalyst for success, particularly for international research scholars embarking on a transformative academic journey. As you navigate the complexities of adapting to a new culture, engaging in rigorous research, and balancing personal and academic responsibilities, defining your long-term goals will provide you with a clear direction and purpose. These goals serve as a beacon, guiding your decisions and actions while instilling a sense of motivation that propels you forward amidst challenges.

In this diverse and dynamic academic environment, it is essential to envision where you want to be in the next five to ten years. Consider the impact you wish to make in your field, the contributions you hope to offer, and the experiences you desire to have. Whether it's publishing groundbreaking research, securing a prestigious position, or developing a network of influential connections, articulating these aspirations will help you create a roadmap that aligns with your values and passions. Remember, your goals are unique to you and shaped by your cultural background, personal experiences, and academic ambitions.

As you establish your long-term goals, embrace the art of flexibility. The journey of research is often unpredictable, filled with unexpected twists and turns. It is essential to remain open to refining your goals as you gain new insights and experiences. This adaptability will not only deepen your understanding of your field but also enhance your resilience in the face of adversity. By allowing your goals to evolve, you can embrace the learning opportunities that arise, transforming potential setbacks into stepping stones toward your ultimate vision.

Moreover, integrating your long-term goals with your personal well-being is crucial in maintaining a healthy work-life balance. As an international scholar, the pressures of academic life can sometimes overshadow your personal needs. Set aside time to reflect on how your goals align with your values and overall well-being. Prioritise self-care, build supportive relationships and engage in activities that rejuvenate your spirit. By nurturing your mental and emotional health, you will not only sustain your motivation but also enhance your capacity to achieve your academic and professional aspirations.

Finally, share your long-term goals with trusted mentors, peers, and life coaches who can provide guidance and support. Engaging in discussions about your aspirations creates a sense of accountability and fosters an encouraging environment. Surrounding yourself with individuals who share your vision can inspire you to stay committed and focused. Remember that achieving long-term goals is not a solitary endeavour; it is a journey best navigated with the support of a community that understands the unique challenges faced by international research scholars. Embrace this journey, and let your aspirations illuminate the path to your success.

Leaving a Legacy in Your Field and in Your Life

Leaving a legacy in your field is a noble aspiration that can shape not only your career but also the landscape of knowledge and innovation in your discipline. This brings us back to the idea of your life purpose, as it is impossible to leave any legacy worth having without a clear definition of the purpose of your life. Anybody on this planet has to define their life purpose at some point in time: it could be being a good family person, a successful business person contributing to the world, a wonderful artist whose work is admired, or simply a good person contributing to wellbeing and happiness of as many people as possible. What makes you happy? In what ways can you create your life purpose and then your legacy?

For international research scholars, this journey begins with recognising the unique perspectives and experiences you bring to your academic community. Your cultural background, research insights, and personal stories can contribute significantly to the richness of discourse within your field. Embracing these aspects allows you to forge a path that resonates with others, inspiring future generations of researchers and academics.

To create a lasting impact, it is crucial to focus on the quality and relevance of your research as well as the contribution to your family and friends and to your community, in big and small ways. Strive for excellence by engaging deeply with your subject matter and remaining committed to integrity and rigour in your work. This dedication not only enhances your own scholarly reputation but also elevates the standards within your discipline. As you produce high-quality research, consider how it can be applied in real-world contexts or how it can address pressing global issues. This approach ensures that your work is not just a collection of papers but a meaningful contribution to society, thereby extending its influence beyond academia.

Your own mentorship plays a vital role in leaving a legacy. Having hopefully benefitted from various mentors and life coaches, you are now in the position to be generous and give yourself. Can you do that? As an international research student, you have the opportunity to guide and support others who may be navigating similar challenges in their academic journeys. Sharing your knowledge, offering advice, and providing encouragement can create a ripple effect, fostering a supportive community of scholars. Take the time to connect with peers, engage in collaborative projects, and participate in discussions that promote growth and knowledge-sharing. By nurturing the next generation of researchers, you solidify your own legacy while empowering others to reach their potential.

Additionally, actively participating in academic networks and professional organisations can amplify your impact. These platforms provide opportunities to share your research, discuss innovative ideas, and connect with like-minded individuals. By presenting your work at conferences, publishing in reputable journals, and engaging in interdisciplinary collaborations, you enhance your visibility and credibility within your field. This engagement not only allows you to leave your mark but also cultivates a culture of collaboration where diverse voices contribute to a more comprehensive understanding of complex issues.

Finally, remember that your life purpose and your legacy are not solely defined by publications or accolades; they encompass the relationships you build and the lives you touch. Cultivating a work-life balance is essential in this pursuit. Prioritise your well-being and mental health, as they are foundational to sustaining your passion and productivity. By modelling a balanced approach to life and work, you inspire others to do the same. Ultimately, leaving a legacy in your field means creating a lasting influence that reflects your values, insights, and commitment to fostering a vibrant academic community.

Exercises:

Creating Vision Boards for Academic Success: Visualising Your Doctoral Graduation and Beyond

Introduction:

Visualisation is a powerful tool for achieving your goals. This exercise will guide you through a meditation designed to help you imagine yourself at your doctoral graduation, confidently stepping into your future as an academic. You'll also visualise yourself working with students and publishing research. This process will help you create a vivid picture of success that can fuel your motivation and drive. We'll begin with grounding and energy work to centre yourself.

Exercise:

1. Find a quiet space where you won't be disturbed. Sit comfortably with your feet flat on the floor. Close your eyes and take three deep breaths, inhaling deeply through your nose and exhaling slowly through your mouth.

2. Begin by grounding yourself: Imagine roots growing from the soles of your feet deep into the earth. Visualise them growing further with every breath you take, anchoring you firmly into the earth below. Feel the strength and stability that comes from these roots as they connect you to the grounding energy of the planet.

3. Now, begin to notice the energy in your body. With each inhale, feel your body filling with light and energy, and with each exhale, release any

tension or stress. Feel your body becoming more energised, balanced, and open.

4. Visualise a warm, golden light entering through the top of your head. See it as a brilliant source of energy, filling you with calm, confidence, and clarity. Let this light move down through your body, energising every cell and expanding outwards until your entire body is glowing with warmth and positivity.

5. Now, with your energy centred and your body fully grounded, begin to visualise yourself at your doctoral graduation. Picture the ceremony—the gown, the cap, and the feeling of accomplishment as you walk across the stage. See yourself receiving your degree and feeling immense pride in this milestone.

6. Next, visualise your future as an academic. Imagine yourself working with students—mentoring them, guiding them through their research, and seeing them grow. Picture yourself teaching a class, presenting your ideas, and watching your students succeed.

7. Visualise yourself publishing your research. Imagine seeing your work in journals, being

referenced by others, and knowing that you have made a lasting contribution to your field.

8. Spend 5-10 minutes in this visualisation, fully immersing yourself in the feelings of accomplishment, purpose, and joy.

9. After the visualisation, write down your reflections:

o What emotions came up during this exercise?

o How did visualising your academic success help you feel more motivated?

o What specific steps can you take to make this vision a reality?

Reflection:
Reflect on the experience and write about any insights or emotions that surfaced. How does it feel to see yourself succeeding in your academic journey? How can you stay connected to this vision as you move forward?

Appendix

Additional Exercises:

--- Exercises for Chapter 1: Embracing the Journey ---

1. Reflect on why you chose to pursue a PhD. Is it driven by personal desire, family expectations, or other factors? Write a paragraph exploring your motivations.

2. Identify three challenges you have faced or anticipate facing as an international scholar. For each challenge, write one strategy to overcome it.

3. Describe how your cultural background influences your academic journey. How can you use this as a strength in your research and personal growth?

--- Exercises for Chapter 2: A Thorough and Comprehensive Exploration of the Various Ways to Define and Understand Success ---

4. Define personal success and academic success in your own words. Reflect on how these definitions align or differ for you.

5. Think about a situation where cultural differences influenced your understanding of success. Write about what you learned from this experience.

6. Create three SMART goals (Specific, Measurable, Achievable, Relevant, Time-bound) related to your research or personal development for the next six months.

REFERENCES

- Akanwa, E.E.,2015.International students in western developed countries: history,challenges,andprospects.J.Int.Stud.5(3),271–284.

- Almurideef R. The challenges that international students face when integrating into higher education in the United States [Internet]. Rowan Digital Works. 2016 [cited 2022 Dec 6]. Available from: https://rdw.rowan.edu/cgi/viewcontent.cgi?article=3338™context=etd.Altinyelken,H.K.,

- Barreto, M., vanBreen, J., Victor, C., Hammond, C., Eccles, A., Richins, M.T., etal.,2022. Exploring the nature and variation of the stigma associated with loneliness. J. Soc.Pers.Relatsh.39(9),2658–2679.

- Barreto, M., Victor, C.,Hammond, C.,Eccles, A.,Richins, M.T.,Qualter, P.,2021.Lonelinessaroundtheworld:age,gender,andculturaldifferencesinloneliness.Pers. Indi-vid.Differ.169,110066.

- Braun, V., Clarke,V., 2020.Onesizefitsall whatcountsasqualitypracticein (reflexive)thematicanalysis?Qual.Res.Psychol.18(3),3

28–352.

- Braun,V.,Clarke,V.,2006.Usingthematicanalysisinpsychology.Qual.Res.Psychol.3(2),77–101.
- Byrne,D.,2021.AworkedexampleofBraunandClarke'sapproachtoreflexivethematianalysis.Qual.Quant.56(3),1391–1412.
- Cacioppo, J.T., Cacioppo, S., Boomsma, D.I., 2013. Evolutionary mechanisms for loneliness.Cogn.Emot.28(1),3–21.
- Choudaha R. Beyond $300 billion: the global impact of international students [Internet]. Studyportals. 2019 [cited 2022Dec24]. Available from: https://file-eu.clickdimensions.com/studyportalscomahg1t/documents/2019_beyond_300breport.pdf?_cldee=8y6r2Eb1R_Eke0K4SFz3OZDXRlmc33LTSE6asrmRI3xHDmZd3OksPXAnHlP1MQS™recipientid=lead-1b66a77b1d81ed1181ad0022489fd956-bc0456549b7c4b0490a2cb565362b0b2™esid=e3afa7e1-b3b4-42d8-92c9-3a9760058bb4.
- Clough,B.A.,Nazareth,S.M.,Day,J.J.,Casey,L.M.,2018.Acomparisonofmentalhealthliteracy,attitudes,andhelpeekingintentionsamongdomesticandinternationaltertiarystudents.Br.J.GuidCouns.47(1),123–

135.

- Cogan N., Chau Y.C.V., Liu X., Kelly S., Anderson T., Flynn C., et al. Understandings of mental health, disclosure, help-seeking and psychological adaptation 9K.

DDepartment of Education, International education strategy: 2021 update: supporting recovery,drivinggrowth[Internet].GOV.UK.2021[cited2022Dec6].Availablefrom:

- Girmay, M., Singh, G.K., 2019. Social isolation, loneliness, and mental and emotional well beingamonginternationalstudentsintheUnitedStates.Int.J.Transl.Med.Res.PublicHealth3(2),75–82.

- Götz,F.M.,Stieger,S.,Reips,U.D.,2018.The emergenceandvolatilityofhomesicknessinexchangestudentsabroad:asmartphonebasedlongitudinalstudy.Environ.Behav.51(6),689–716.

- Hasnain, A., Hajek, J., 2022. Understanding international student onnectedness. Int. J.Intercult.Relat.86,26–35.HESAHighereducationstudentstatistics:UK,2020/21-wherestudentscomefromandgotostudy[Internet].

- HESA.2022[cited 2022 Dec6]. Available from:

- https://www.hesa.ac.uk/news/25-01-2022/sb262-higher-education-student-statistics/location.
- Hillman N. The costs and benefits of international higher education students to the UK economy [Internet]. HEPI. 2021 [cited 2022 Dec6]. Available from: https://www.hepi.ac.uk/2021/09/09/the-costs-and-benefits-of-international-higher-education-students-to-the-uk-economy/
- Hoek, L., Jiang, L., 2019.Improvingthepsychosocialwellbeingofinternational students: the relevance of mindfulness.
- https://pubmed.ncbi.nlm.nih.gov/36035251/.
- https://www.gov.uk/government/publications/international-education-strategy2021-update/international-education-strategy-2021-update-supporting-recovery-driving-growth.Ellard,O.B.,Dennison,C.,Tuomainen,H.,2022. Review:interventionsaddressinglonelinessamongstuniversitystudents:asystematicreview.ChildAdolesc.Ment.Health.
- Hunley, HA., 2010. Students'functioningwhile studyingabroad: The

impact of psychologicaldistressandloneliness.InternationalJournalofInterculturalRelations.34(4), 386–392.

- J.Soc.Clin.Psychol.16(3),277–298.
- J.Stud.Int.Educ.12(2),148–180. Serrano Sánchez,J.,Zimmermann,J.,Jonkmann,K.,2021.ThrillingtravelorLonesomeLongHaul?lonelinessandacculturationbehaviorofadolescentsstudyingabroad.Int.J.Intercult.Relat.83,1–14.
- Li,Y.,Liang,F.,Xu,Q.,Gu,S.,Wang,Y.,Li,Y.,etal.,2021.SocialSupport,attachment closeness,andself-esteemaffectdepressionininternationalstudentsinChina.Front.Psychol.12.
- Liu, T., Wong, Y.J., Tsai, P.-.C, 2016. Conditional mediation models of intersecting identities among female Asian International Students. Couns. Psychol. 44 (3), 411–441.
- Masi, C.M., Chen, H.-.Y., Hawkley, L.C., Cacioppo, J.T., 2010. A meta-analysis of interventions to reduce loneliness. Pers. Soc. Psychol. Rev. 15 (3), 219–266.
- McClelland,H.,Evans,J.J.,Nowland,R.,Ferguson,E.,O'Connor,R.C,2020.Lonelinessasapredictor

of suicidal ideation and behaviour: a systematic review and meta-analysis of prospective studies. J. Affect. Disord. 274, 880–896.

- Meet the Trustworthiness Criteria. Int. J. Qual. Methods 16(1), 1609406917733847.

- Miret, M., 2018. Association of Loneliness with all-cause mortality: a meta-analysis.

- Morris, A., Mitchell, E., Wilson, S., Ramia, G., Hastings, C, 2021. Loneliness within the home among international students in the private rental sector in Sydney and Melbourne. Urban Policy Res. 40(1), 67–81.

- Nowell, L.S., Norris, J.M., White, D.E., Moules, N.J., 2017. Thematic Analysis: striving to

- Oei, T.P., Notowidjojo, F., 1990. Depression and loneliness in overseas students. Int. J. Soc. Psychiatry 36(2), 121–130.

- Park, C., Majeed, A., Gill, H., Tamura, J., Ho, R.C., Mansur, R.B., et al., 2020. The effect of loneliness on distinct health outcomes: a comprehensive review and meta-analysis. Psychiatry Res. 294, 113514.

- Perlman, D., Peplau, L., 1981. Toward a social psychology of loneliness. In: Personal

Relationships inDisorder.AcademicPress,London,pp.32–56.

- PLoSONE13(1).Roitblat,Y.,Cleminson,R., Kavin,A.,Schonberger,E.,Shterenshis,M.,2017.Assessment of anxiety in adolescents involved in a study abroad program: a prospective study.Int.J.Adolesc.Med.Health32(2).
- Rathakrishnan, B., Bikar Singh SS, Kamaluddin, M.R., Ghazali, M.F., Yahaya, A., Mohamed,N.H.,etal.,2021.Homesicknessandsocio-culturaladaptationtowardsperceivedstressamonginternationalstudentsofapublicuniversityinsabah:anexplorationstudyforsocialsustainability.Sustainability13(9),4924.
- Rico-Uribe, L.A., Caballero, F.F., Martín-María, N., Cabello, M., Ayuso-Mateos, J.L.,
- Saravanan,C.,Mohamad,M.,2019.AliasA. Copingstrategiesusedbyinternationalstudentswhorecoveredfromhomesicknessanddepressioninmalaysia.Int.J.Intercult.Relat.68,77–87.
- Sawir,E.,Marginson,S.,Deumert,A.,Nyland,C.,Ramia,G.,2007.Lonelinessandinternationalstudents:anAustralianstudy
- Shan,C.,Hussain,M.,Sargani,G.R.,2020.A

mix-methodinvestigationonacculturativestressamongPakistanistudentsinChina.PLoSONE15(10).

- Solmi,M,Veronese,N,Galvano,D,Favaro,A,Ostinelli,EG,Noventa,V,etal.,2020.Factors associated with loneliness:A numbrella review of observational studies. Journalof Affective Disorders.271,131–138.

- Toh,G.,Pearce,E.,Vines,J.,Ikhtabi,S.,Birken,M.,Pitman,A.,etal.,2022.Digitalinterventionsforsubjectiveandobjectivesocialisolationamongindividualswithmentalhealthconditions:ascopingreview.BMCPsychiatry22(1),331May12.

- Tong, A., Sainsbury, P., Craig, J., 2007. Consolidated criteria for reporting qualitative research(COREQ):a32-itemchecklistforinterviewsandFocusGroups.Int.J.Qual.HealthCare19(6),349–357.

- Victor,C.,Qualter,P.,Barreto,M.,2019.Whatisloneliness:insightsfromtheBBClone-linessexperiment.Innov.Aging3(Supplement_1).

- Wawera,A.-.S.,McCamley,A.,2019.Lonelinessamonginternationalstudentsintheuk.J.Furth.High.Educ.44(9),1262–1274.

- Wiseman, H., 1997. Faraway from home: the loneliness experience of overseas students.
- Yang, K., Victor, C., 2011. Age and loneliness in 25 European nations. Ageing Soc. 31(8), 1368–1388.
- Zheng, S. Johnson, R. Jarvis et al Current Research in Behavioral Sciences 4(2023)100113 among Asian international students studying in Scotland: a sequential multimethod study [Preprint]. 2021 [cited 2023 Jan 10]. Available from: https://strathprints.strath.ac.uk/79851/1/Cogan_psychological.pdf.

www.ingramcontent.com/pod-product-compliance
Lightning Source LLC
Chambersburg PA
CBHW061726070526
44583CB00024B/3022